CONFIDENT
ASSESSMENT
in HIGHER EDUCATION

Sara Miller McCune founded SAGE Publishing in 1965 to support the dissemination of usable knowledge and educate a global community. SAGE publishes more than 1000 journals and over 800 new books each year, spanning a wide range of subject areas. Our growing selection of library products includes archives, data, case studies and video. SAGE remains majority owned by our founder and after her lifetime will become owned by a charitable trust that secures the company's continued independence.

Los Angeles | London | New Delhi | Singapore | Washington DC | Melbourne

CONFIDENT
ASSESSMENT
in HIGHER EDUCATION

Rachel Forsyth

Los Angeles | London | New Delhi
Singapore | Washington DC | Melbourne

Los Angeles | London | New Delhi
Singapore | Washington DC | Melbourne

SAGE Publications Ltd
1 Oliver's Yard
55 City Road
London EC1Y 1SP

SAGE Publications Inc.
2455 Teller Road
Thousand Oaks, California 91320

SAGE Publications India Pvt Ltd
B 1/I 1 Mohan Cooperative Industrial Area
Mathura Road
New Delhi 110 044

SAGE Publications Asia-Pacific Pte Ltd
3 Church Street
#10-04 Samsung Hub
Singapore 049483

Editor: James Clark
Assistant editor: Diana Alves
Production editor: Rachel Burrows
Copyeditor: Sarah Bury
Proofreader: Brian McDowell
Indexer: Adam Pozner
Marketing manager: Lorna Patkai
Cover design: Naomi Robinson
Typeset by: C&M Digitals (P) Ltd, Chennai, India
Printed in the UK

Library of Congress Control Number: 2022933943

British Library Cataloguing in Publication data

A catalogue record for this book is available from
the British Library

ISBN 978-1-5297-7081-0
ISBN 978-1-5297-7080-3 (pbk)

At SAGE we take sustainability seriously. Most of our products are printed in the UK using responsibly sourced
papers and boards. When we print overseas we ensure sustainable papers are used as measured by the PREPS
grading system. We undertake an annual audit to monitor our sustainability.

CONTENTS

ABOUT THE AUTHOR

Rachel Forsyth is an educational developer who currently works at Lund University in Sweden as a project manager. She was previously Head of the University Teaching Academy at Manchester Metropolitan University, where she was involved in major institutional change projects, particularly in relation to inclusive learning communities and assessment in higher education. She is a Principal Fellow of the Higher Education Academy (HEA) and has taught on postgraduate programmes for teaching in higher education for twenty years, including leading a specialist module on assessment. She was a member of the Degree Standards Project team from 2017 to 2021, which explored sector-owned processes for professional development of external examiners in the UK. As Editor-in-Chief of the *Student Engagement in Higher Education Journal* for five years, she is an active member of the Researching, Advancing, Inspiring Student Engagement (RAISE) network committee.

ACKNOWLEDGEMENTS

I have learned so much about assessment from so many people that it feels invidious to identify individuals, but my discussions over many years with Rod Cullen, Mark Stubbs, Neil Ringan, Ron Hamilton and Patrick Gannon at Manchester Metropolitan University have helped to shape many of the ideas in this book. I have also had the enormous privilege of learning from colleagues on the UK Degree Standards Project team between 2017 and 2022, particularly Sue Bloxham, Pete Boyd, Corony Edwards, Andy Lloyd, Erica Morris, Berry O'Donovan, Margaret Price, Nicola Reimann, Chris Rust, Ian Sadler, Geoff Stoakes, and Ruoyu Yuan.

James Clark from Sage Publishing suggested this book, and Diana Alves has kept me on track and provided patient and timely support throughout the process. Stephanie Aldred, Bartek Buczkowski, Peter Gossman, Claire Hamshire, Chris Little, Amanda Miller, Orlagh McCabe, Charles Neame, and Stephen Powell are all kind colleagues who acted as critical readers, but the responsibility for remaining errors rests entirely with me.

I want to thank Claire Hamshire and Janet Lord for providing moral support for years, making sense of what is going on, and reminding me not to take things entirely seriously. Their ability to find the right gif for any situation is unrivalled.

And finally, it would be impossible to name the many colleagues over the years who have asked me questions about assessment and forced me to engage with the whole assessment lifecycle so that I could develop my own confidence in thinking about assessment. I hope the book helps you to develop answers of your own: only you can design the best assignment task for your students.

PART 1

IDENTIFYING THE CHALLENGES

The observation that assessment in higher education has changed very little over time is frequently made, and partially accurate. Assignment tasks which were commonplace in the nineteenth century, such as essays and unseen examinations, are still present in many university curricula, but alongside them, you will now also find many examples of what is often called authentic assessment, such as business presentations, scientific posters, false teeth, or men's shoes. The landscape can be varied and exciting, but it is fair to say that making changes to assessment can be a daunting task, with multiple stakeholders to satisfy and apparently complex regulations. This book aims to guide you through the process of making decisions about assessment on your own **modules**, and Part 1 sets the scene for this by identifying the challenges and contexts which you need to consider before beginning your planning.

A note about vocabulary

Throughout the book, I will use the word 'teachers' to describe those who work directly with students to plan, facilitate and assess their learning. There are many other names in English for this role (professor, lecturer, tutor) which others may prefer.

To improve readability, the nouns 'assessment' and 'assignment' may be used interchangeably when relating to tasks set for students. 'Course' and 'programme' will also be used interchangeably, and 'module' will refer to a component of a programme or course. Finally, the word 'marking' will generally be used to describe the process of judging student work – you may prefer 'grading', and they are interchangeable.

A glossary is also provided for other commonly used assessment terms and words in the glossary are shown in bold on first use.

1

ASSESSMENT IN HIGHER EDUCATION

Chapter overview

This chapter explores:

- The reluctance to discuss assessment
- Terminology in common use and some of the purposes of assessment in higher education
- The complexity of assessment systems in higher education
- Treating assessment as a 'wicked' problem

Introduction

This chapter provides a general introduction to assessment in higher education, covering common principles and processes and considering how assessment is managed in different countries and higher education contexts. It is intended to set the scene for discussion about ways to address the challenges faced in higher education assessment, which are considered in the rest of this book. It should provide a useful primer for those new to assessment in higher education; some of it may cover familiar ground for experienced assessors, but it should still be a useful review.

Assessment in Higher Education

Assessment of student learning is a key aspect of all forms of education that lead to a qualification or other recognition of achievement. It can be a complex and fraught topic, associated with anxiety and pressure for both **teachers** and students. Boud (1995) considers the ways in which assessment is used as a control mechanism in assessment; while he focuses on the control of student behaviours, it also has a powerful effect on teachers.

There are differences between its effect in compulsory and higher education. Control factors in compulsory education tend to be extrinsic; teachers are more likely to be working towards common national or regionally mandated assessment of their students, often by **examination**, and which they have not seen themselves. The idea of a common assessment for all students at the same stage is intended to show equivalence of standards across the cohorts, and independence in grading.

By comparison, teachers assessing in the higher education context are likely to be setting the assessments for their own students. This means that they are less constrained in relation to the content and style of assessment, and can theoretically begin with a blank sheet of paper for each assignment task they design. In practice, this freedom brings with it a different set of concerns and skill requirements, and challenges in demonstrating the equivalence of standards. Having all of the responsibility for the assessment implies the need to take great care in the design of the tasks and the ways they are graded. University teachers may feel bound by disciplinary or institutional rules, anxious about maintaining standards, uncertain or unsupported in making changes, or simply too short of time to do anything different from previous years. There is also a requirement to be able to demonstrate comparability of performance with assessors in other universities, so that the qualifications achieved by students from different institutions may be considered equivalent.

This book aims to provide those responsible for assessment in higher education with a basis for making confident and sustainable decisions that are workable for students, teachers, and universities, and maintain the academic standards expected by wider society. The scope of that sentence indicates the complexity and challenge of the task; by considering the role of individuals, teaching teams, and organisational structures, the book seeks to make the challenge accessible and attractive to all stakeholders.

Making space to talk about assessment

The invisible task

What kind of image comes to mind when you are asked to visualise higher education activity? Judging from the kind of stock images provided in university prospectuses or brochures for educational software, you are expected to think of a professor standing in front of a whiteboard, or even a blackboard, or someone sitting with their books in a library. It is fairly commonplace to hear about good, or bad, teaching. Students may be overheard talking about lectures and, during the coronavirus pandemic in 2020–22, the UK government regularly commented on the inferior quality of online teaching compared to on-campus lectures. Staff in higher education are likely to be observed regularly in the classroom and to receive **feedback** on their teaching, although it is still fair to say that much teaching happens behind closed doors.

Assessment doesn't usually figure in these depictions of university. Is this because assessment may conjure more negative images: a harassed teacher grading a set of exams, an anxious student trying to finish an essay, or maybe giving a presentation, working with an employer to solve a real-life problem, carrying out a simulated clinical procedure, or any other assessment-related situation? Admittedly, it may simply be that such examples may be less photogenic.

Those university brochures talk about the content of what the student will learn, and what they might achieve afterwards. They might mention how students will learn, in state-of-the-art buildings with integrated technology. They will probably, in the UK at least, indicate briefly what kind of **assessment task** students might expect (usually generalised to a choice between examination or continuous assessment through **coursework**). It is less likely that students will find a description of how they will be supported to undertake the assessment, even though these tasks will be the way in which achievement as a student is ultimately judged.

A lack of visual representation might also be because nobody wants to emphasise this part of university life, which is often associated with anxiety for both students and staff. If we seek out mention of assessment more specifically, we might find that photographs of examination rooms might be used in newspaper articles about university assessment, possibly bemoaning the erosion of standards, or we might see pictures of jubilant graduating students, celebrating their success by launching their hats into the air. Whilst this book is not about the semiotics of assessment, the absence of symbolic representation reflects the fact that there is little general conversation about the design and management of assessment compared to discussion of teaching in higher education.

A solitary pursuit

Another possible reason for the low profile of assessment in higher education could be that it is often considered as a solitary pursuit both for students and for their tutors. Students are mostly set individual assignments by which teachers judge their personal performance; talking to peers about these assignments is a sensible thing to do, in terms of personal and professional development, but there may be hint of collusion if this discussion becomes public. In some cases, there may be a competitive edge to the assessment which precludes sharing ideas with others. Or perhaps the assessment is being completed at the last minute, under pressure, and the student feels alone in this challenge.

Once students have done their part and completed their assigned work, marking (grading) of assignments is largely done by individual tutors working alone. There are exceptions, such as when marking event-based activities such as presentations, performances, or exhibitions, but reviewing students' work may be seen as something one locks oneself away to complete. It may also be presented by tutors as a difficult and unpleasant chore to be completed before other, more engaging, activities may ensue. This image of assessment as a practice which is carried out behind closed doors and endured by all parties is at odds with modern ideas of inclusive curriculum design, digital collaboration, transparency, authenticity, and professional practice.

Assessment as a negative part of university life

Perhaps we don't like to discuss assessment because it is often mentioned in negative terms. Student satisfaction with assessment and feedback is considerably lower than it is with other aspects of their experiences in higher education, according to the UK National Student Survey (Office for Students, 2021), which means that it tends to be seen as something pulling against the creation of a happy learning environment.

There is a nervousness about experimentation in assessment in higher education which manifests itself at both an individual and institutional level. Creative and innovative teaching practices may attract praise, but when assessment is discussed in the media, it is often in the context of 'dumbing down', with the suggestion that assessments are getting easier over time, or that qualifications in less familiar subject areas, or from more recently established universities, hold less value than those which are more traditional. This creates an anxiety about change, even though the student satisfaction data suggest that new approaches might be a good idea.

In the UK, many university policies dictate the range of types and sizes of assessment task which may be set, and these rules place constraints on curriculum design. These restrictions are not a requirement of the UK's regulatory regime, which is actually agnostic about these factors, but the perceived link between traditional assignment types and rigour is difficult to break.

Confidence to discuss assessment

There is little conversation about these apparent inconsistencies, whether within institutions or outside them, for instance in disciplinary networks. My personal experience of working with teachers in higher education and prospective **examiners** indicates to me that there is a general lack of confidence in teachers' own ability to design, support, use, and evaluate assessment as an integral part of their higher education practice, and that they often feel unsupported in making changes because of a perception of rigid university processes and procedures. This book aims to encourage conversation and build confidence in relation to assessment, primarily with higher education staff, but also, through them, with students. More openness and discussion about assessment practices should provoke critical engagement with the decision-making processes associated with assessment, opening these up to proper debate and building confidence in both individual autonomy and institutional support.

The book begins by reviewing the purposes and practices of assessment in higher education, before going on to consider the challenges and constraints, and moving on to practical suggestions for becoming a more confident assessor.

Terminology

Assessment literacy

This handy phrase is one for which the meaning seems self-evident, but in fact is quite difficult to define. We will use it in the book to refer to a fluent understanding of the vocabulary, principles, and purposes of assessment and the ability to make informed and confident decisions about the design and management of assessment.

Learning outcomes and assessment

Learning outcomes describe what a student will be able to do at the end of a course of study. They are used to help people understand what will be taught and assessed during the **course**, and this makes them useful for students who are interested in studying the subject, for teachers who are planning teaching, for administrators who are setting up the course structures, and for external examiners or auditors who may be reviewing the academic standards and expectations of the course.

At their simplest, assessable learning outcomes include two key elements (Carroll, 2001):

1 An action verb to describe the behaviour (what the student will do) which demonstrates the student's learning.
2 Information about the context for the demonstration.

Programme-level outcomes

The **award** of a qualification to a student means that they have been assessed against all of the learning outcomes specified for that programme (or course). For a full programme such as a diploma, bachelor's or master's degree, these outcomes will usually be quite generic. For some subject areas, such as history, mathematics, or philosophy, they may be very broad in scope (Table 1.1, examples 1–3). In other disciplines, outcomes may be influenced or specified by an external professional organisation which provides accreditation, such as for medicine, accountancy, engineering, architecture, or law, and these programme-level outcomes may be quite specific (Table 1.1, examples 6–8). In some countries, their use may be optional, and in others, they may form a key part of the national system of describing, managing, and auditing academic standards. If you aren't sure how programme outcomes are used, ask colleagues, and if they aren't sure, you could try asking someone in your university who works with university regulations in a department, such as a quality office or registry, or in an academic development office.

Table 1.1   Examples of programme learning outcomes. Square brackets represent the addition of an element which is specific to the subject area

On successful completion of this programme, students will be able to:

1   Analyse relevant literature [in the subject area]
2   Design a research project to investigate a question [in the subject area]
3   Reflect on their own practice and create a professional development plan
4   Analyse the needs of a client and recommend a course of action
5   Express themselves through the creation of novel art works
6   Make a clinical diagnosis based on [a range of tests] and recommend a course of treatment
7   Safely prescribe medication [for a particular purpose]
8   Prepare an argument for a defence client

Module-level outcomes

Learning outcomes are also used to describe what students will be able to do at the end of shorter periods of study. Most programmes of study that lead to an award in higher education are quite long – often three to four years for a bachelor's degree, or one to two years for a master's. To make courses more manageable, they are broken down into smaller sections, or modules. Each module in a **programme of study** can have its own learning outcomes and these are of course more specific than the programme-level outcomes. They also reflect the expectations for the stage at which that module is studied in relation to the whole programme.

An outcome for the first module on a bachelor's programme will reflect the fact that students are being inducted into university work:

On successful completion of this module, the student will be able to:

• Define the basic concepts of [a specific topic in the subject area]
• Summarise literature from [a specific topic in the subject area]
• Explain the differences between [different schools of thought in the subject area]

At the end of the programme, the students will be expected to have more analytical skills:

> On successful completion of this module, the student will be able to:
> - Critically analyse results of experiments undertaken to investigate [a specific topic in the subject area]
> - Evaluate the effect of [a specific topic in the subject area] on [a generic topic in the subject area]

The learning outcomes for the first unit on a master's programme may combine an introduction to the subject matter with an expectation that the students bring with them an ability for critical analysis from their first degree:

> On successful completion of this module, the student will be able to:
> - Identify and evaluate contemporary issues [in the subject area], citing appropriate evidence in support
> - Critically examine the impact of contemporary issues [in the subject area] on specific organisations and individuals

The master's dissertation or major project, at the end of the course, will bring together complex expectations, such as synthesis and complex project planning, and so the learning outcomes will demonstrate synthesis and original research, such as in this example:

> On successful completion of this module, the student will be able to:
> - Specify an appropriate research question [in the subject area]
> - Design an appropriate project to collect and analyse primary data in an ethical and effective way
> - Analyse primary and secondary data in a way which addresses the research question
> - Communicate effectively in a written form appropriate to the audience

These module learning outcomes are key to all the decisions subsequently taken about assessment; each module is usually assessed using individual assessment tasks which demonstrate achievement of the outcomes and lead to the award of **credits** for each successful module completion. It is thus important to understand module structures in relation to the confident design and organisation of assessment.

There are variations between national systems, of course, but there has been a general trend towards modularisation, with an award being composed of a set number of credits. The number of credits allocated to an individual module may be set by the individual university, or there may be a nationally-used structure. On the European Credit Transfer System (ECTS), for instance, a bachelor's degree requires a total of 180 credits. This may be mapped to a different structure in each European country, but there is a system for comparing the credits in each country. In the US, a four-year college degree (bachelor's) will usually require around 120–128 semester credit hours. India expects 120 credits for an undergraduate degree, Australia awards degrees when 144 credit points are achieved.

It would be usual to link these module credits to a notional amount of student effort, measured in hours. Studies have shown that there is wide variability between the amount of time successful students spend on module assessments (Darmody et al., 2008; Kember, 2004), but an idea of the time expected is useful for both the student in planning their work and for the teacher planning the teaching, and for the size and nature of the assessment task to be completed.

All of this is important to the teacher in deciding what should be covered in an assessment task, and what their expectations of the students are. The articulation of learning outcomes is also clearly important in considering the purpose of the assessment.

Taxonomies of learning outcomes

A taxonomy of learning outcomes provides a way of categorising outcomes, which can be useful in looking at patterns of expectations across a programme, or across a series of modules. For instance, you might use them to review whether the programme has enough outcomes covering core knowledge, or practical skills. They can also be useful for identifying language that is suitable for writing outcomes. The two most commonly used taxonomies in higher education, generally referred to as Bloom's (Bloom, 1956) and SOLO (Biggs & Collis, 1982) respectively, also include a hierarchy of outcomes, with students progressing through levels of the model. You can see the influence of this thinking in national frameworks for grading, such as those in the UK (QAA, 2014).

Bloom's Taxonomy

While this model is still commonly known as Bloom's, it is more usual to use a revised version produced by Anderson and Krathwohl (2001) which puts more emphasis on creativity as the pinnacle of achievement (Figure 1.1). It is commonly used to support the writing of learning outcomes, by associating each level with action verbs. For instance, 'knowledge' might be associated with verbs such as describe, select, or list; 'create' might be associated with design, plan, or revise. You can find plenty of lists of verbs associated with this taxonomy on the internet.

SOLO taxonomy

The SOLO taxonomy (Figure 1.2) can be used both for the creation of outcomes in the same way as Bloom's Taxonomy, by associating each level with certain verbs: 'pre-structural' probably wouldn't feature in higher education outcomes, as it is associated with knowing nothing about the topic, but 'unistructural' might be linked to list and describe, while 'relational' could be linked to explain, estimate, validate (and many other examples). The categories in this taxonomy can also be used to judge the whole of a student's **submission** and to support grading.

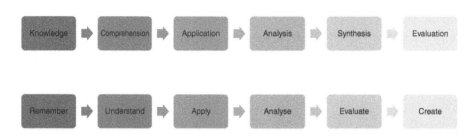

Figure 1.1   Bloom's taxonomy (Bloom, 1956) (top) and Krathwohl's adapted version (Anderson & Krathwohl, 2001) (bottom)

Figure 1.2   SOLO taxonomy (Biggs & Collis, 1982)

Formative and summative assessment

Formative assessment is generally considered to be assessment which does not count for module credits, as opposed to **summative assessment**, which does. Formative assessment is integrated into teaching, and in this book we will discuss it in relation to planning teaching, in Chapter 7. Unless there is explicit reference to formative, all references to assessment can be assumed to be about summative tasks.

Approaches to marking

There are four main approaches to marking that you may encounter in higher education. The one you are most likely to come across is outcome-based, but it is worth knowing about the others so that you can identify their use. You may also find them useful for formative assessment.

Outcome-based or criterion-referenced

The student submission is judged against the intended outcomes, using criteria related to the outcomes, and without considering any other factors. This is the approach we will focus on in the book, partly because the outcomes approach is required in many national systems, and partly because the other approaches are difficult to apply in the modularised systems found in contemporary higher education.

Norm-referenced

Student work is marked and then ranked in order from best to worst, and a fixed proportion of students is given a grade from each possible grade band. This is a fairly familiar approach in the compulsory education sector when tens of thousands of students are sitting the same assessments. The idea is that it smooths out differences in individual markers and in the **validity** of tasks from year to year. It relies on large numbers of results for this smoothing to be effective, and it doesn't actually assess performance against set outcomes, although if the tasks are well designed, it should come close. In general, it is not suitable for higher education with small numbers of students completing each assignment task.

Comparative judgement

The idea is that it is easier to judge relative merit than to mark directly against criteria (Thurstone, 1927, cited in van Daal et al., 2019). You compare two submissions at a time, and decide which is better, rather than allocating a grade. You then review a third submission, and decide where that sits in relation to the first two, and place that one in the right place in the order, and so on. At the end of the process, you have all of the submissions ordered from best to worst. Pollitt (2012) suggests that the use of adaptive comparative judgement removes the need to design tasks which can be marked reliably, because of its focus on validity, but a heavy time investment is needed, and grades will still need to be allocated at the end of the process, perhaps using a norm-referenced scheme. There has been some work done in using it to compare marker judgements as a form of **moderation** without using grades, and we will touch on this in Chapter 6.

Ipsative

Students are marked according to their improvement since the last assessment, so it is a form of comparative judgement, but used for two pieces of the student's own work (Hughes, 2011). It is quite difficult to see how this can be used for summative assessment, but it may be a motivating inclusion to formative feedback.

The purposes of assessment

One of the reasons that thinking and talking about assessment practices causes anxiety is that it may be difficult to agree what their underlying purpose is. It is possible for a single assignment task to be expected to serve several, if not all, of the purposes listed in Table 1.2, which is not an exhaustive list, nor is it in any order of importance or desirability.

Table 1.2 Multiple purposes of assessment

To judge current competence	To judge current knowledge	To judge capacity for future learning
To encourage focus on particular aspects of the curriculum	To reward the meeting of teacher expectations	To accredit a minimum level of professional competence
To differentiate performance among students	To validate the effectiveness of teaching	To permit progression to the next level of study
To permit award of a final qualification	To demonstrate maintenance of academic standards	To identify areas for individual future development
To recognise an ability to follow instructions	To recognise the ability to perform under pressure	To confirm that intended learning outcomes have been achieved
To build student confidence	To reduce the number of students on the course	To judge teacher competence in preparing students for assessment

Boud (2000, p. 159) introduced the notion that assessment always does 'double duty' to capture this inherent tension, and to emphasise the need to attend to all potential purposes. There are many ways in which these tensions manifest themselves, and they both influence and are influenced by the perspectives of the different people who have a stake in the outcome of the assessment: students, teachers, quality managers, auditors, future employers, professional bodies, and so on. Harman and McDowell (2011) suggest that these tensions lead to a constant renegotiation of identity for both teachers and students as they move through different parts of the assessment process. This shifting of perspective can be uncomfortable, and may be another reason why assessment is discussed less often than teaching.

Any approach to assessment therefore needs to consider a variety of purposes. Some of these purposes may seem contradictory. For instance, an external body might require a timed, unseen examination to permit award of a professional qualification, while the teacher might think that completion of an authentic case study over a two-day period is a more realistic test of professional competence. You may also think that some of the purposes listed in Table 1.2 are undesirable, and that you want to ensure that they are specifically excluded from planning.

Teachers need to consider how they prioritise different purposes in designing assignment tasks. Students may have a different view of the importance of these factors in deciding the value they will personally gain from a particular task and how much effort they should put into it. Boud's (2000) identification of these tensions, and his proposal to consider assessment as a complex system rather than trying to identify a single purpose, has been very influential in encouraging more expansive discussions of assessment design. We will return to these tensions when we look at the design of assessment tasks in Chapter 5.

Assessment as, of, and for learning

One way of trying to put order on this situation of multiple purposes is to consider three broad purposes: assessment of, as, and for learning.

Assessment of learning

The phrase 'assessment of learning' is often synonymous with summative assessment, and thus linked to credit acquisition, using our previous definition of summative assessment. Another way to look at it is that it is generally used to refer to the functional, rather than the developmental, purposes of assessment. If judging achievement is its sole purpose, there is no need for the teacher to provide developmental feedback, suggesting how students might improve in the future.

Assessment as learning

There is interesting polarity in the literature about the meaning of this term. The benign version is that the processes of assessment, if well designed, can support student learning by improving their ability to self-assess and regulate their study, and empower students to take some control of their responses to assessment (Dann, 2014; Rodríguez-Gómez & Ibarra-Sáiz, 2015). In this scenario, assessment is a natural consequence of the learning process, as students ask for and receive feedback to develop their ideas; formative assessment is really important in this approach, because it helps the students to learn about process as well as the product, which is the summative assessment.

An alternative view is that assessment as learning represents too much of a focus on learning outcomes, and criterion-based assessment disempowers students and teachers because of the intense focus on achievement (Torrance, 2007). The critique is based on observations that students ask for and receive feedback focused on passing the assignment rather than on developing their skills. Learning is not an intellectual and valuable pursuit in its own right, but must be linked to achievement. In that case, formative assessment exists merely to prepare students for their final assignment tasks.

Assessment for learning

Black et al. (2004, p.10) define assessment for learning as 'any assessment for which the first priority in its design and practice is to serve the purpose of promoting students' learning'. In this approach, assessment exists to support learning and the developmental aspects of feedback take priority over everything. In practice, assessment for learning is often thought of as being synonymous with formative assessment in which students are being prepared for a summative assignment. In Chapters 5 and 7, we will also look at how feedback, a key part of the assessment process, can be used for learning.

The full logical consequence of saying that the only purpose of assessment is to support learning would be to remove grades from the summative assessment process, a practice known as 'ungrading' (Blum & Kohn, 2020; Stommel, 2018). This is a pretty daunting prospect for most teachers, and inconceivable in any institution that actually awards qualifications, but it makes for an interesting thought experiment to consider what it would mean to remove grades and whether it would be desirable in your context. If you weren't thinking about grades, would you make different choices about the assessment design? What impact would it have on your relationships with students? Would they engage with your assessments?

Assessment as a wicked problem

It is tempting to think that one could try to put some order on the list in Table 1.2, by categorising the purposes using these definitions, i.e. for, of, and as learning. For some of the purposes, this looks pretty simple: 'To permit award of a final qualification' is surely assessment *of* learning, while 'To identify areas for individual future development' is probably assessment *for* learning, although it might be assessment *as* learning, depending on the context. The concept of double duty means that this quickly becomes a difficult task, driven by a need to determine which of assessment of, for, or as learning is the dominant approach.

Rather than try to narrow the focus or espouse a single set of definitions, in this book we will instead accept the complexity of assessment purpose and provide tools for analysing and selecting assessment tasks and approaches to grading and feedback which fit the particular situation you are encountering at the time. This means treating assessment as a wicked problem.

A wicked problem, according to Rittel and Webber (1973), is one which, among other characteristics, is unique, poorly defined, has many stakeholders with potentially conflicting values, and has no single correct solution. Addressing a wicked problem requires the practitioner to continually monitor what is happening, to continue to consult with stakeholders, to work with others to make sense of the problem, and to adapt behaviours and actions to reflect the current situation (Jordan et al., 2014). In previous work, Alicia Prowse and I (Prowse & Forsyth, 2017) have suggested that considering assessment as a wicked problem would free teachers from searching, or sticking with, a mythical correct approach, allowing them to choose a solution which provides the best fit in a particular situation. The process of managing a wicked problem also requires the use of constant evaluation and engagement with enhancement of the situation, with reference to the views and experiences of stakeholders.

This characterisation, although it sounds complex, can free up the teacher and other stakeholders in thinking about assessment. Letting go of the belief that there is a single correct answer provides the permission to come up with a good solution to a particular assessment situation. It also makes it essential to consider the purposes, priorities, and perspectives of all stakeholders and to engage in persuasive argument where needed to achieve change.

The process in Figure 1.3 provides a structure for working with a wicked problem. It breaks the process of solving the problem into manageable but essential steps.

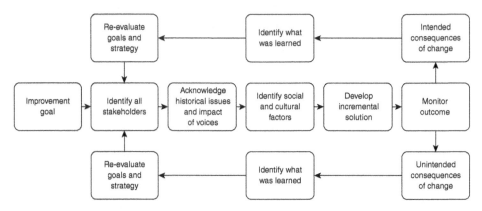

Figure 1.3   General model for wicked problem management (Hamshire et al., 2019)

Table 1.3   Application of wicked problem-solving approach in designing a new assessment approach

Improvement goal	Replacement of timed, unseen examination with a timed, authentic case study completed in a realistic time (two days)
Identify all stakeholders	External body administrators, students, previous graduates, teachers in other universities
Acknowledge historical issues and impact of voices	Identify purposes of existing assessment; review current research on authentic assessment; initiate discussion with colleagues in other universities (e.g. through mailing lists or at conferences)
Identify social and cultural issues	'This is how we've always done it'; consider practical issues around fairness, integrity, grading
Develop incremental solution	If the case study still seems like a good approach, set the case study as a formative assessment; and share the student work with the professional body and colleagues at other universities
Monitor outcomes	Gather evaluation on the formative work from stakeholders
Identify what was learned	Revisit the intended aim of the change, and the original assessment purposes to check that they have been met, and nothing has been lost
Re-evaluate goals and strategy	Work with external body to pilot a summative version of the assessment

To exemplify this, let's return to the previous example of the external body which holds to the idea that a timed, unseen exam is best, which is at odds with the view of the teacher, who would like to set an authentic case study set in a realistic professional environment. There is a considerable imbalance of power in this situation: the external body is a gatekeeper to a professional qualification; a single teacher in a single university may feel there is no clear route to suggest change. Table 1.3 breaks down the steps an individual could take to persuade the external body of the value of their idea. This is a complex example with many stakeholders, but the approach can be applied elsewhere, and we will look at other situations in the second half of the book.

The assessment lifecycle

Some of the complexities around assessment come from trying to think about assessing as a single process, which must be completed in the same way for all tasks at all levels. This kind of thinking can lead to the dominance of a single type of assessment task, such as essays, or unseen examinations, or an artistic artefact, because they can be set and completed in a replicable and consistent way. These are valid ways to assess, of course, but they may not serve all of the purposes of assessment intended by the course team.

A dependence on one or two methods of assessment may also make it easier for some groups of students to achieve well, because they learn and assimilate the rules of these types of tasks, whereas others may struggle with the constraints and would do equally well if there were other ways to demonstrate their achievements.

A counter-argument here is that reducing the number of types of assessment allows students to develop mastery of an approach. This is a valid argument if the development of a skill such as, say, writing a legal report is a significant part of the intended outcomes of the course, and other means of expression (perhaps making a legal argument, or interviewing a client, in the same disciplinary context) are not considered to be as important. If it is important for students to develop skills in different forms of communication, and/or the course is intended to allow students to identify and develop their own approaches to learning and voices in which to express their thinking, then there is a strong argument for offering a variety of assessment tasks.

One way to tackle the complexity of assessment design is to plan each assessment task individually. If we do this, it is possible to choose a different combination of purposes for each task, and then make choices about the design of the task description, grading arrangements, and feedback strategy which are appropriate to the task itself. We will look at a process for doing this called the assessment lifecycle (Figure 1.4). This technique combines the wicked problem-solving approach with practical suggestions for each stage of assessment design.

Using the lifecycle approach means that you can consider each aspect of a particular task in relation to the stakeholders, previous experiences, best practice, and new research, using the wicked framework. The full range of an individualised approach to assignment tasks may be difficult to implement in different national and institutional situations, or as an early career teacher. However, every teacher will have control over some part of an assessment task, and so can begin to improve their own part of the process and recommend changes to colleagues and students.

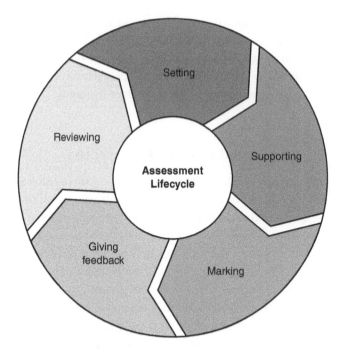

Figure 1.4 Assessment lifecycle

Source: Adapted from Forsyth et al. (2015)

Conclusion

Assessment in higher education is complex and there is no single best answer to any of the challenges of assessment design. This could be an opportunity for creative thinking around assessment. In the remaining chapters in this section, we will explore the landscape of assessment in the contemporary university, considering some of the challenges faced by teachers designing and practising assessment in higher education. This will lead us to consider ways in which to demystify and destress the process of planning and managing assessment, and perhaps even aspire to make it enjoyable.

Further reading

Price et al (2012) provides a great deal more detail on the concept of assessment literacy and its relationship to student engagement and learning.

If you need a refresher on the purposes of education, and of your role as a teacher, to help with thinking about your purposes in assessment, it's always worth revisiting the manifestos of Biesta (2014), Freire (1972), and hooks (1994), although they are all focused on teaching and say little about assessment *per se*.

Bloom's original book (1956) on his taxonomy may give you a sense of his intended use of these kinds of frameworks.

References

Anderson, L. W., & Krathwohl, D. R. (Eds.). (2001). *A taxonomy for learning, teaching and assessing: A revision of Bloom's Taxonomy of educational objectives: Complete edition*. New York: Longman.

Biesta, G. (2014). *The beautiful risk of education*. Boulder, CO: Paradigm.

Biggs, J. B., & Collis, K. F. (1982). *Evaluating the quality of learning: The SOLO taxonomy (Structure of the Observed Learning Outcome)*. New York: Academic Press.

Black, P., Harrison, C., Lee, C., Marshall, B., & Wiliam, D. (2004). Working inside the black box: Assessment for learning in the classroom. *Phi delta kappan, 86*(1), 8–21.

Bloom, B. (1956). *Taxonomy of educational objectives: The classification of educational goals*. Chicago, IL: Susan Fauer Company.

Blum, S. D., & Kohn, A. (2020). *Ungrading: Why rating students undermines learning (and what to do instead)*. Morgantown, WV: West Virginia University Press.

Boud, D. (1995). Assessment and learning: Contradictory or complementary? In P. Knight (Ed.), *Assessment for learning in Higher Education* (pp. 35–48). London: Kogan Page.

Boud, D. (2000). Sustainable assessment: Rethinking assessment for the learning society. *Studies in Continuing Education, 22*(2), 151–167.

Carroll, J. (2001). Writing learning outcomes: Some suggestions. Retrieved 08/02/08 from www.brookes.ac.uk/services/ocsd/2_learntch/writing_learning_outcomes.html

Dann, R. (2014). Assessment as learning: Blurring the boundaries of assessment and learning for theory, policy and practice. *Assessment in Education: Principles, Policy & Practice, 21*(2), 149–166.

Darmody, M., Smyth, E., & Unger, M. (2008). Field of study and students' workload in higher education: Ireland and Austria in comparative perspective. *International Journal of Comparative Sociology, 49*(4–5), 329–346.

Forsyth, R., Cullen, R., Ringan, N., & Stubbs, M. (2015). Supporting the development of assessment literacy of staff through institutional process change. *London Review of Education, 13*(34–41).

Freire, P. (1972). *Pedagogy of the oppressed*. London: Penguin.

Hamshire, C., Jack, K., Forsyth, R., Langan, A. M., & Harris, W. E. (2019). The wicked problem of healthcare student attrition. *Nursing Inquiry*. https://doi.org/10.1111/nin.12294

Harman, K., & McDowell, L. (2011). Assessment talk in design: The multiple purposes of assessment in HE. *Teaching in Higher Education, 16*(1), 41–52. www.informaworld.com/10.1080/13562517.2010.507309

hooks, b. (1994). *Teaching to transgress: Education as the practice of freedom*. New York: Routledge.

Hughes, G. (2011). Towards a personal best: A case for introducing ipsative assessment in higher education. *Studies in Higher Education, 36*(3), 353–367. https://doi.org/10.1080/03075079.2010.486859

Jordan, M. E., Kleinsasser, R. C., & Roe, M. F. (2014). Wicked problems: Inescapable wickedity. *Journal of Education for Teaching, 40*(4), 415–430. https://doi.org/10.1080/02607476.2014.929381

Kember, D. (2004). Interpreting student workload and the factors which shape students' perceptions of their workload. *Studies in Higher Education, 29*(2), 165–184. www.informaworld.com/10.1080/0307507042000190778

Office for Students. (2021). *National Student Survey results.* www.officeforstudents.org.uk/advice-and-guidance/student-information-and-data/national-student-survey-nss/get-the-nss-data/

Pollitt, A. (2012). The method of Adaptive Comparative Judgement. *Assessment in Education: Principles, Policy & Practice, 19*(3), 281–300. https://doi.org/10.1080/09695 94X.2012.665354

Price, M., Rust, C., O'Donovan, B., Handley, K., & Bryant, R. (2012). *Assessment literacy: The foundation for improving student learning.* ASKe, Oxford Centre for Staff and Learning Development.

Prowse, A., & Forsyth, R. (2017). Global citizenship education – assessing the unassessable? In I. Davies, L.-C. Ho, D. Kiwan, C. Peck, A. Peterson, E. Sant, & Y. Waghid (Eds.), *The Palgrave Handbook of Global Citizenship and Education.* London: Palgrave.

QAA. (2014). *The frameworks for higher education qualifications of UK degree-awarding bodies.* London: Quality Assurance Agency for Higher Education. www.qaa.ac.uk/docs/qaa/quality-code/qualifications-frameworks.pdf

Rittel, H. W., & Webber, M. M. (1973). Dilemmas in a general theory of planning. *Policy Sciences, 4*(2), 155–169.

Rodríguez-Gómez, G., & Ibarra-Sáiz, M. S. (2015). Assessment as learning and empowerment: Towards sustainable learning in higher education. In *Sustainable learning in higher education* (pp. 1–20). Cham, CH: Springer International.

Stommel, J. (2018). *How to ungrade.* www.jessestommel.com/how-to-ungrade/

Thurstone, L. L. (1927). A law of comparative judgment. *Psychological Review, 34*(4), 273.

Torrance, H. (2007). Assessment as learning? How the use of explicit learning objectives, assessment criteria and feedback in post-secondary education and training can come to dominate learning. *Assessment in Education, 14*(3), 281–294.

van Daal, T., Lesterhuis, M., Coertjens, L., Donche, V., & De Maeyer, S. (2019). Validity of comparative judgement to assess academic writing: Examining implications of its holistic character and building on a shared consensus. *Assessment in Education: Principles, Policy & Practice, 26*(1), 59–74. https://doi.org/10.1080/09695 94X.2016.1253542

2

WHAT DO WE NEED TO TALK ABOUT?

Chapter overview

This chapter explores:

- Validity, reliability, and fairness
- The role of academic judgement
- Disparities in student achievement
- Factors affecting academic judgement
- Coping with uncertainties in assessment

Introduction

In Chapter 1, we focused on the purposes of assessment in higher education, and the complexity of planning and managing assessment in relation to these. The assessment lifecycle was introduced to provide a systematic approach to looking at the different stages of the design and management of assessment. In this chapter, we will focus on principles of assessment and some key factors which might affect assessment in higher education.

Principles of assessment

To begin with, we need to introduce the principles of validity, **reliability**, and **fairness**.

Validity

An assessment is valid if it measures what it was intended to measure. As we saw in Chapter 1, this usually means that an assignment task on a higher education course is considered to be valid if it assesses the **intended learning outcomes**.

Reliability

An assessment is reliable if repeated measurements lead to the same outcome. This is easy to conceptualise if you are, for example, weighing out ingredients for a recipe or checking the length of a piece of wood for a craft project. In assessment of students, 'reliability is demonstrated when different markers make the same judgement or when one marker makes consistent judgements about a piece of work at different times' (Bloxham & Boyd, 2007, p. 38). This sounds sensible, but in practice it is difficult to achieve, partly due to the multiple purposes we considered in Chapter 1. We will therefore return to the challenge of reliability in assessment throughout this chapter.

Fairness

An assessment is fair if all students have an equal opportunity to demonstrate their achievement of the intended outcomes. In order to achieve this, fairness needs to be considered at each stage of the assessment lifecycle.

The role of academic judgement

When we talk about marking students' work, we use the term 'academic judgement' regularly. It is often used in official documentation – for example, in the UK Quality Code (QAA, 2018) – as shorthand for the process of academic decision-making. It is important to think about this concept of judgement and the ways in which teachers develop the expertise and confidence to mark students' work.

It has been a reasonable generalisation in most, if not all, countries, to say that the qualification to be employed as a university teacher has been to have a recognised proficiency and knowledge in the subject which is being taught. The required expertise may have been developed from some combination of research, scholarship, and professional experience. Demonstrable competence in teaching was not always an expectation.

As a result, students may have had very mixed experiences in relation to both teaching and assessment. When participation in higher education was limited and students were often drawn from the same social classes as their teachers, they may have managed to cope with this variability because of their familiarity with cultural codes and expectations, or by having enough confidence to ask questions. However, it is also likely that many students failed assignments and left their studies early; in the UK, national data were not collected systematically on students' failure to progress until 2003, when such information became part of a set of performance indicators and, since this date, there has been considerable scrutiny of these statistics.

There is a clear link to assessment here, in that students may leave university early because they fail their assignments, but it should be noted that there are many other reasons why students leave higher education before they have completed their intended programmes of study, as Hillman (2021) points out: ill-health, having chosen the wrong course, financial difficulties, and so on. The topic of student persistence in higher education has been extensively studied (to find out more, you could start with Ahmed et al., 2014; Hamshire et al., 2019; Jones, 2008; Thomas, 2013; Tinto, 2006; Webb & Cotton, 2018). In this book we will focus particularly on the role of assessment in student progression and success.

In order to mark students' work, university teachers need detailed subject knowledge, and an understanding of the intended learning outcomes for the course. They also need to be familiar with the appropriate national standards for the subject area and level of study, and with institutional and professional expectations for marking procedures. All of these elements are combined into a process of decision-making which is generally referred to as academic judgement.

Academic judgement is not something that is easily taught to new university teachers. It depends on the individual acquisition of a considerable body of tacit knowledge, which is frequently developed through informal mentoring and discussion with colleagues. Sometimes, if not often, new teachers may be expected to work through marking a set of submissions with no particular support other than the existing course documentation, such as course and module specifications, or **assignment briefs**.

The development of tacit knowledge about marking is based on a variety of sources and experiences. It is situated within the context of the discipline and of the institution. For example, demonstrating creativity in a submission for a fine art course would be a basic expectation for a student to pass, but in an accountancy degree, it might gain the highest grades (or even, conversely, lead to a fail, depending on the context of the creativity). A medical qualification is likely to assess breadth of factual knowledge via a huge number of multiple-choice questions, while a fine art student may need to design a single, complex show to synthesise what they have learned.

Tacit knowledge is also likely to be influenced by personal experiences and values. If you or someone you know has had bad experiences with assessment, such as feeling your grade or feedback were unfair, or not understanding the instructions, you might feel motivated to do things differently with your own students. If you were really successful with unseen examinations, you might regard them as the best way to assess students in your subject. Of course, you might mitigate these views with reference to research on assessment and so develop your knowledge further.

Your values and beliefs may also be a factor in decision-making. How do you see your role in higher education? Are you working in a university primarily to create new knowledge, to maintain standards, to develop the next generation of colleagues, to contribute to social justice? What are your views on the purposes of assessment? Do you view assessment primarily as an activity to measure progress, to provide a door which must be unlocked before the student can continue, to identify gaps in knowledge, to celebrate achievement? There are no simple, or correct, answers to these questions; they are part of the composite description of you as an assessor of complex student work. It is useful to be aware of these potential influences on your decision-making when you are reflecting on your practice. You may already be wondering about the impact of academic judgement on the reliability of assessment, and we will naturally return to this point as we work through the stages of assessment design in Chapters 5 to 7.

Disparities in student achievement

When we analyse assessment outcomes, such as final grades and likelihood of progressing from one academic stage to the next, we find that students with certain characteristics tend to perform less well than those with other characteristics. In the UK, the starkest national evidence of this came in a report (UUK/NUS, 2018) which showed an average gap in attainment of 13.2% between white students and students who identified as being from other ethnic groups. While there is variation in these student groups between institutions, and between courses within the same institutions, the gap is measurable and persistent. Controlling for a range of other student characteristics, such as previous qualifications, does not explain the difference. Students who enter higher education with similar educational achievements are more likely to achieve a higher grade if they are white. This situation is known as the award gap.

Similar gaps have been noted in other countries where these data are collected; for instance, in South Africa, there was a gap of almost 9% between the percentages of black and white South African students who passed their courses in 2015 (Department of Higher Education and Training, 2017). Other student characteristics also appear to have an effect on attainment outcomes; disabled students tend to do less well than non-disabled students (Office for Students, 2019). An internal analysis at a large UK university showed that students who apply for additional financial support, compared to those who do not, and students who continue to live in the family home, compared with those who live in student accommodation, also do less well (private communication). In the US, studies of first-generation students (those who are the first in their family to attend higher education) have shown that they are more vulnerable to early departure (Ishitani, 2003; Mehta et al., 2011; Strayhorn, 2007).

These unexplained differences are identified in the final stage of the assessment cycle (Figure 1.4), reviewing. One element of this review would involve looking across all of the assessment outcomes for individual students. This provides a useful reminder of the importance of carrying out thorough reviews of all assessments; action to address disparities will come from careful attention to the design of each assignment task and we will build this into Part 2 of the book.

There are many ways to filter these data, and a strong likelihood of intersectional complexity which can make it difficult to pinpoint exact reasons for these attainment differences. However, in whatever ways the data are organised, they show that assessment outcomes may not be fair, and that this is something which assessors need to acknowledge and to challenge in their practice. Given that it can be safely assumed that assessors in higher education intend to assess with validity, reliability, and fairness, we will consider this in further discussion of assessment design.

Subjectivity and variability

It is easier to confront the uncomfortable facts of the award gaps mentioned above if you believe that assessment in higher education is inevitably associated with variability and unintended subjectivity. This is not because assessors are carrying out their work badly, or wrongly. It is because the assessment of higher-level skills, knowledge, and understanding is inherently complex, and we all bring different expectations, values, and experiences to the tasks of designing and managing assessment.

Assessment tasks in higher education are intended to provide opportunities for students to analyse, synthesise, and evaluate their learning. Students are expected to provide their own interpretations of what they have observed, read, and experienced; it is inevitable that they will produce complex submissions which do not always fit an anticipated model. At all stages of the assessment lifecycle, judgement is required to make sure that the assessment task and the criteria used to grade the student work will test the intended outcomes, are set at an appropriate level, allow for student interpretation, and maintain academic standards.

In most cases, marking criteria must be designed to accommodate a range of possible approaches and solutions. This means that criteria may be quite broad, and subject to interpretation, so different assessors may come to different decisions when they are assessing the same piece of work. There are some possible exceptions for topics which can be codified, such as mathematical formulae or practical protocols, which we will look at in more detail when considering individual tasks. This variability is a difficult concept for many teachers in higher education to accept, but study after study has shown that it is the case (Baume et al., 2004; Bloxham, den-Outer, et al., 2015; Butler Shay, 2004; Hanlon et al., 2005; Orr, 2010; Price, 2005).

The possibility of subjectivity and variability provides a reasonable explanation for many of the challenges faced by assessors in higher education. Let's think about the award gap again from this perspective. The design of an assessment task and its criteria need to be broad enough to make it both challenging and original, and is therefore associated with inherent subjectivity in making judgements. There is a strong possibility that tutor expectations, which help them to come to a judgement about the piece of work submitted by the student, are not surfaced clearly enough in the description and criteria. As well as differences between tutors, it is probable that students will also interpret the task description and the criteria in different ways depending on their previous experiences and perspectives. Those students who think in similar ways to the teachers, have had similar educational experiences, or are able to ask the right questions to elicit these expectations, might be more likely to produce a piece of work which achieves a high grade. It is also possible that students who have experience of different educational systems, or have had a gap before returning to education, or who just have different ways of approaching problems, may submit work which receives a low grade. This is often characterised as the 'hidden curriculum' (Sambell & McDowell, 1998), although this term also has broader connotations than simply referring to assessment. These are unintentional effects which may lead to unfair outcomes.

There are approaches which can be used to reduce variability between assessors and to make assessor intentions more explicit, which we will look at in more detail later. For the moment, it is just important to accept the strong possibility of subjectivity and variability, and to be open-minded about some aspects of assessment which you may be accustomed to thinking about as unchangeable.

Academic integrity

It was mentioned earlier that a valid assessment measures what it is intended to measure; an important consideration in this definition is that the submission must represent the work of the student who will receive credit for the assessment. Assessment cannot be valid, reliable, or fair if this is not the case. The phrase 'academic integrity' is frequently used to summarise the values we expect of students in relation to assessment. Five values have been associated with this phrase by the Centre for Academic Integrity at Clemson University in the USA (Fishman, 2014): accuracy, honesty, fairness, responsibility, and respect. In relation to assessment, these values mean that we expect students to create their own work and to acknowledge the work of others. Conventionally, this is done by using citations to show where they are referring to the published work or views of others.

Many institutions in North America ask their students to sign up to honour codes which confirm their commitment to these or similar sets of values. It is also generally expected that assessors will exhibit these values in relation to their part of the assessment lifecycle.

This definition of academic integrity is based on the positive demonstration of values, which is a difficult concept to measure. The phrase 'academic misconduct' is often used to describe the situation when one or more of these values is absent or ignored. Academic misconduct is usually subject to penalties such as a reduction in marks, a requirement to resubmit the work, or even expulsion from study. There are three specific types of misconduct which a teacher in higher education is likely to come across in relation to assessment: **plagiarism**, **contract cheating**, and cheating in examinations.

Plagiarism

Plagiarism is the act of presenting someone else's ideas or work as your own. This covers a range of practices from paraphrasing ideas to copying small or large pieces of another's work without acknowledgement. In many universities, it also includes re-using parts of your own work in similar ways for different assessments; this is known as self-plagiarism, and its inclusion in the definition is intended to stop students gaining credit for a second piece of work without having learned anything new.

While copying from a classic of the subject area may be relatively easy to spot, a busy assessor grading open-ended tasks (those which don't have defined answers) to a tight deadline may find it difficult to detect small extracts of work from multiple sources, or work which has been submitted for marking in other contexts. We will look at ways to support assessors in the identification of assessment misconduct at different stages of the assessment lifecycle in Part 2.

Contract cheating

When we talk about contract cheating, we are referring to the practice of a student paying someone else to produce an assignment, and then submitting it as if they had completed it themselves (Clarke & Lancaster, 2006, cited in Lancaster & Clarke, 2016).). It is a form of plagiarism, as someone else's work is being passed off as one's own.

While asking someone else to complete an assignment has probably always happened, a considerable contract cheating industry has developed alongside online shopping technology and improved digital tools (Bretag et al., 2019; Rigby et al., 2015). Students can type in the title and details of an assignment task and a deadline, and they will receive an immediate offer and a price tailored to the request. The companies that offer these services are likely to say that they are providing an 'example' for students to use when developing their own work, to cover themselves against potential legal action. The quality of the products is variable (Sutherland-Smith & Dullaghan, 2019), which might be what you would expect, but the underlying issue is academic integrity and the consequent effect on the validity of the assessment. There is also growing evidence of contract cheating companies blackmailing students after the purchase of their 'services', by reporting their activity to universities (Sutherland-Smith & Dullaghan, 2019; Yorke et al., 2020).

There is some evidence that assessors have a slightly better than even chance of detecting contract cheating (Dawson & Sutherland-Smith, 2017), but the continued existence of so-called 'essay mill' websites suggests that it is likely to be a problem in most disciplinary areas. Again, we will look at ways to mitigate this later.

Cheating in examinations

By definition, an examination is an assessment carried out under controlled conditions: the time allowed to complete the task is controlled, there is limited choice about the task, and students are usually supervised by specially employed staff to make sure that they do not make reference to anything which is not allowed while taking the examination: these staff may be referred to as **proctors** or **invigilators**. These constraints are intended to reduce the likelihood of cheating, and to make the conditions equivalent for all students. Cheating in physical examinations is still possible despite the supervision: before people had widespread access to portable technology, reminders written on arms or hidden up sleeves were said to be frequently used, and today there is a market for hidden devices such as earpieces and smart watches which can be used for reference to notes or even help from another person. It is probably wise to assume that cheating is possible and to think about how to design the exam questions so that help from outside is not so useful – we will look at this in detail in Part 3.

External pressures

The discussion above presents assessment as an important academic activity, which needs regular review and reflection among peers. Most assessment decisions will be made among academic colleagues reviewing data and student experiences at a local level, with some institutional and external oversight of processes and outcomes. It is also important to consider the role of a range of external stakeholders who may have views on processes and outcomes. They can exert strong influence on general decision-making in universities, which in turn may influence what happens at the level of an individual assessment.

National or regional quality organisations

In most countries, there is an organisation which provides some general oversight of the quality and standards of university courses. In the UK, the Quality Assurance Agency performs this role, publishing a Quality Code (QAA, 2018) which provides a framework for managing higher education quality and standards. Other examples are the Swedish Higher Education Authority, the Australian Tertiary Education Quality and Standards Agency, and the South African Council on Higher Education. In the USA, such organisations operate at state level. In some countries, such as France, quality assurance may be distributed among different departments depending on the type of institution. The same bodies, or linked ones, may regulate university powers to award qualifications and design new ones.

These organisations are likely to review university-level data about admissions, student progression, and satisfaction, and use this to provide further instructions or advice. Depending on national priorities, they may also have additional requirements; in the UK, there is follow-up on student career development after they have graduated, to try to assess the value of qualifications via graduate employment. UK universities are also expected to have a plan for widening participation and ensuring fair access to learning for all students.

National and regional organisations are unlikely to be involved in the details of course and assessment design, but they may set out general principles which will be interpreted into guidelines by each university. In some countries, particular types of assessment may be required as part of these principles but, in general, universities in most countries enjoy a great deal of autonomy over assessment. As a teacher designing and grading university assignments, you will probably have scope for flexibility and creativity in your assessment practice.

You are more likely to be directly affected by the work of such external organisations on the occasions when they are influenced by government policies or media interest in a particular topic. For example, during the coronavirus pandemic in 2020–22, it was impossible for school-leavers or university students in the UK to sit timed, unseen, examinations. This led to a great deal of discussion in the media about alternatives; the UK government stated its position that unseen, timed, examinations are the fairest way to assess students and that other forms of assignment task would be inferior. There is no clear evidence for this position, but its statement was influential with the national regulatory bodies, and this translated into a wish to maintain some form of unseen examination wherever possible.

National or regional organisations may also have views about academic standards and perceived variations between universities. These may lead to measures to compare or manage standards between institutions; for instance, in the UK, there is the external examiner system, where teachers from other universities review assessment processes and outcomes for each other.

These kinds of discussions about standards may become more political in nature; they may have a more direct impact on individual teacher assessments than more general frameworks, if they lead to relatively sudden changes in policies and practice.

Professional organisations

Professional organisations provide another layer of regulation and oversight to university courses. Professions such as accountancy, architecture, dentistry, education, engineering, law, medicine, or nursing are likely to have an awarding body which specifies standards.

In some countries, this may be affiliated to the national organisations mentioned above, but, in others, they will be entirely independent of government. The role of these organisations is to support the profession by describing expected standards, representing the interests of qualified professionals, and in some cases, accrediting university courses by agreeing that they meet the standards expected in the profession.

These types of organisation may wish to review the details of the course, including the ways in which assignment tasks are designed and graded. It is worth remembering that their core purpose is to represent the interests of the profession, and they may not employ educational experts who understand assessment; you may need to be prepared to explain the rationale for your assessment choices. There is wide variation in the approaches professional bodies take, but they will provide documentation when they have specific expectations of assessments on the courses which lead to registration in their profession. As a teacher on a course which is linked to one of these organisations, you are likely to be a member of the profession yourself, and so familiar with the expectations of your peers. You may find that you have to follow certain expectations about assignment tasks, such as the type or length, but the body may equally leave these features to academic judgement. Before starting on the design of an assessment on a course which is subject to external body accreditation, find out what the parameters are and how much flexibility is possible. Professional organisations will usually have an education or accreditation officer who should be happy to discuss this with you.

Uncertainty

All of the factors we have considered above lead inevitably to the conclusion that grading of student work is subject to some uncertainty. In science, uncertainty refers to the possible variation of a measurement from the 'true' value; it gives a sense of the accuracy of measurements and the estimated size of this variation is always provided alongside the measurement itself. Uncertainty is not the same thing as making a mistake in the measurement; the uncertainty arises from the accuracy of the measuring instrument and measurement processes.

There are accepted methods of estimating uncertainty, which are based on repeating the measurement many times and carrying out a statistical analysis of the difference from the mean result. In this chapter, we have introduced a great deal of uncertainty about assessment of students; the scientific idea of repeating the 'measurement' (grading the work) is not always available and may not be reliable. If the same grader marks the same student submission several times, do they always bring the same academic judgement to the work? Could they somehow forget what they had seen the first time they marked the work?

The closest similarity to a repeated measurement in science would be for multiple graders to mark a piece of work, and for a mean mark to be calculated. A modified version of this process is undertaken in national examinations in the compulsory education sector in many countries to try to standardise academic judgement and to quantify the uncertainty in grading, and to identify questions which may be particularly prone to variation in assessor judgement. It is not practical to do this for individual assessments in universities, although we will look at ways to improve consistency in academic judgement in Chapters 5 and 7.

Uncertainty can be reduced by improving the instrument and the process. One solution to the problem of uncertainty in assessment is to design an assignment task which is perfectly reliable; this would be one where we know that the student cannot copy someone else's answer, where every assessor will always make the same academic judgement, and where there are no factors which affect the students' ability to prepare for and complete the assessment. From reading these two first chapters, you will probably rapidly conclude that this is not a viable possibility in higher education. You might be able to fulfil the 'no copying' by having an unseen examination taken under strict conditions; you could ensure that the assessor will always make the same judgement by assessing objective facts only; you would need to make sure that a student with a disability which prevents them from handwriting in examination conditions has someone to dictate to. These solutions are possible, but would the resulting assignment task achieve the purposes set out in Chapter 1?

Moderation

Moderation is one way to mitigate some of the uncertainties associated with an individual assignment task. It is a term which will be familiar in some national contexts, and less so in others. It seems to be quite difficult to define. Sadler (2013, p. 5) offers a description of process: 'Moderation is intended to ensure that the mark a particular student is awarded is independent of which marker does the marking.' He goes on to describe it as a consensus-seeking activity. This is echoed by another definition from Australia: 'a practice of engagement in which teaching team members develop a shared understanding of assessment requirements, standards and the evidence that demonstrates differing qualities of performance' (Adie et al., 2013, p. 968). Bloxham et al. (2015, p. 638) provide a loose definition as 'a taken-for-granted approach to agreeing, assuring and checking standards', while for Crimmins et al. (2016, p. 428), moderation is a 'collective process of meaning making or learning, a social process of creating understanding'. These definitions all point towards the creation of socially agreed standards which aim to reduce the uncertainty we have considered. We will use the term to mean critical peer review of assessment processes and procedures, including review of a sample of student submissions, which can be completed at module or programme level.

As Sadler (2013) points out, moderating a group of markers on an individual task aims to ensure consistent grading across student submissions for that particular task, and the repeated process of moderation improves our ability to interpret criteria and make judgements. Thus, in itself the activity of moderation is key to our own development of assessment literacy in the context of our disciplinary areas. Moderation has been found to be an important way to reduce variability between assessors (Ecclestone, 2001; Hanlon et al., 2005). Further discussion of the practicalities of moderation can be found in Chapter 6.

Conclusion

Uncertainty in assessment is almost inevitable. This can be troubling but, as with scientific measurement, it can be mitigated and managed. As we continue to look at assessment design, we will consider the ways in which we can reduce uncertainty and increase validity, reliability, and fairness across the assessment lifecycle.

Further reading

Many of these ideas are discussed in more detail in two important books which lay the foundation for scholarly consideration of all aspects of assessment in higher education (Bloxham & Boyd, 2007; Price et al., 2012).

In addition, Bloxham, Hughes, and Adie (2015) is a good way to find out more about different practices which have been labelled as moderation, and their limitations and possible negative impact in relation to equity and standards.

It is also worth reading the 2018 report on disparities in student achievement in the UK (UUK/NUS, 2018). While the situation is bound to be different in other countries, and many countries don't collect this kind of data anyway, it raises questions which should be asked everywhere.

References

Adie, L., Lloyd, M., & Beutel, D. (2013). Identifying discourses of moderation in higher education. *Assessment & Evaluation in Higher Education*, 38(8), 968–977. https://doi.org/10.1080/02602938.2013.769200

Ahmed, N., Kloot, B., & Collier-Reed, B. I. (2014). Why students leave engineering and built environment programmes when they are academically eligible to continue. *European Journal of Engineering Education*, 1–17. https://doi.org/10.1080/03043797.2014.928670

Baume, D., Yorke, M., & Coffey, M. (2004). What is happening when we assess, and how can we use our understanding of this to improve assessment? *Assessment & Evaluation in Higher Education*, 29(4), 451–477.

Bloxham, S., & Boyd, P. (2007). *Developing effective assessment in Higher Education: A practical guide*. Maidenhead: Open University Press/McGraw Hill.

Bloxham, S., den-Outer, B., Hudson, J., & Price, M. (2015). Let's stop the pretence of consistent marking: Exploring the multiple limitations of assessment criteria. *Assessment & Evaluation in Higher Education*, 1–16. https://doi.org/10.1080/02602938.2 015.1024607

Bloxham, S., Hughes, C., & Adie, L. (2015). What's the point of moderation? A discussion of the purposes achieved through contemporary moderation practices. *Assessment & Evaluation in Higher Education*, 1–16. https://doi.org/10.1080/02602938.2015.1039932

Bretag, T., Harper, R., Burton, M., Ellis, C., Newton, P., Rozenberg, P., Saddiqui, S., & van Haeringen, K. (2019). Contract cheating: A survey of Australian university students. *Studies in Higher Education*, 44(11), 1837–1856.

Butler Shay, S. (2004). The assessment of complex performance: A socially situated interpretive act. *Harvard Educational Review*, 74(3), 307–329.

Clarke, R., & Lancaster, T. (2006). Eliminating the successor to plagiarism? Identifying the usage of contract cheating sites. In Proceedings of *2nd International Plagiarism Conference*, Newcastle-Upon-Tyne, June 2006, Northumbria Learning Press.

Crimmins, G., Nash, G., Oprescu, F., Alla, K., Brock, G., Hickson-Jamieson, B., & Noakes, C. (2016). Can a systematic assessment moderation process assure the quality and integrity of assessment practice while supporting the professional development of casual academics? *Assessment & Evaluation in Higher Education*, 41(3), 427–441. https://doi.org/10.1080/02602938.2015.1017754

Dawson, P., & Sutherland-Smith, W. (2017). Can markers detect contract cheating? Results from a pilot study. *Assessment & Evaluation in Higher Education*, 1–8. https://doi.org/10.1080/02602938.2017.1336746

Department of Higher Education and Training. (2017). *Statistics on post-school education and training in South Africa: 2015*. www.dhet.gov.za/DHET%20Statistics%20Publication/Statistics%20on%20Post-School%20Education%20and%20Training%20in%20South%20Africa%202015.pdf

Ecclestone, K. (2001). 'I know a 2:1 when I see it': Understanding criteria for degree classifications in franchise university programmes. *Journal of Further and Higher Education*, 25(3), 301–312.

Fishman, T. (Ed.). (2014). *The fundamental values of academic integrity*. Clemson University. www.academicintegrity.org/wp-content/uploads/2017/12/Fundamental-Values-2014.pdf.

Hamshire, C., Jack, K., Forsyth, R., Langan, A. M., & Harris, W. E. (2019). The wicked problem of healthcare student attrition. *Nursing Inquiry*. https://doi.org/10.1111/nin.12294

Hanlon, J., Jefferson, M., Molan, M., & Mitchell, B. (2005). *An examination of the incidence of 'error variation' in the grading of law assessments*. www.education.uwa.edu.au/__data/assets/pdf_file/0006/1888611/Hanlon.pdf

Hillman, N. (2021). *A short guide to non-continuation in UK universities*. www.hepi.ac.uk/wp-content/uploads/2021/01/A-short-guide-to-non-continuation-in-UK-universities.pdf

Ishitani, T. T. (2003). A longitudinal approach to assessing attrition behavior among first-generation students: Time-varying effects of pre-college characteristics. *Research in Higher Education*, 44(4), 433–449.

Jones, R. (2008). *Student retention and success: A synthesis of research*. York: Higher Education Academy.

Lancaster, T., & Clarke, R. (2016). Contract cheating: The outsourcing of assessed student work. *Handbook of Academic Integrity*, 639–654.

Mehta, S. S., Newbold, J. J., & O'Rourke, M. A. (2011). Why do first-generation students fail? *College Student Journal*, 45(1), 20–36.

Office for Students. (2019). *Beyond the bare minimum: Are universities and colleges doing enough for disabled students?* www.officeforstudents.org.uk/media/1a263fd6-b20a-4ac7-b268-0bbaa0c153a2/beyond-the-bare-minimum-are-universities-and-colleges-doing-enough-for-disabled-students.pdf

Orr, S. (2010). We kind of try to merge our own experience with the objectivity of the criteria: The role of connoisseurship and tacit practice in undergraduate fine art assessment. *Art, Design & Communication in Higher Education, 9*(1), 5–19. http://dx.doi.org/10.1386/adch.9.1.5_1

Price, M. (2005). Assessment standards: The role of communities of practice and the scholarship of assessment. *Assessment & Evaluation in Higher Education, 30*(3), 215–230. www.informaworld.com/10.1080/02602930500063793

Price, M., Rust, C., O'Donovan, B., Handley, K., & Bryant, R. (2012). *Assessment literacy: The foundation for improving student learning.* ASKe, Oxford: Oxford Centre for Staff and Learning Development.

QAA. (2018). *The revised UK Quality Code for Higher Education.* London: Quality Assurance Agency for Higher Education. www.qaa.ac.uk/quality-code

Rigby, D., Burton, M., Balcombe, K., Bateman, I., & Mulatu, A. (2015). Contract cheating & the market in essays. *Journal of Economic Behavior & Organization, 111*, 23–37. https://doi.org/http://dx.doi.org/10.1016/j.jebo.2014.12.019

Sadler, D. R. (2013). Assuring academic achievement standards: from moderation to calibration. *Assessment in Education: Principles, Policy & Practice, 20*(1), 5–19. https://doi.org/10.1080/0969594X.2012.714742

Sambell, K., & McDowell, L. (1998). The construction of the hidden curriculum: Messages and meanings in the assessment of student learning. *Assessment & Evaluation in Higher Education, 23*(4), 391–402. https://doi.org/10.1080/0260293980230406

Strayhorn, T. L. (2007). Factors influencing the academic achievement of first-generation college students. *Journal of Student Affairs Research and Practice, 43*(4), 1278–1307.

Sutherland-Smith, W., & Dullaghan, K. (2019). You don't always get what you pay for: User experiences of engaging with contract cheating sites. *Assessment & Evaluation in Higher Education*, 1–15. https://doi.org/10.1080/02602938.2019.1576028

Thomas, L. (2013). What works? Facilitating an effective transition into higher education. *Widening Participation and Lifelong Learning, 14*, 4–24. https://doi.org/10.5456/WPLL.14.S.4

Tinto, V. (2006). Research and practice of student retention: What next? *Journal of College Student Retention: Research, Theory & Practice, 8*(1), 1–19.

UUK/NUS. (2018). *Black, Asian and Minority Ethnic student attainment at UK universities: #closingthegap.* Universities UK/National Union of Students. www.universitiesuk.ac.uk/policy-and-analysis/reports/Pages/bame-student-attainment-uk-universities-closing-the-gap.aspx

Webb, O. J., & Cotton, D. R. E. (2018). Early withdrawal from higher education: a focus on academic experiences. *Teaching in Higher Education, 23*(7), 1–18. https://doi.org/10.1080/13562517.2018.1437130

Yorke, J., Sefcik, L., & Veeran-Colton, T. (2020). Contract cheating and blackmail: A risky business? *Studies in Higher Education*, 1–14. https://doi.org/10.1080/03075079.2020.1730313

3

WHAT ELSE SHOULD
WE TALK ABOUT?

Chapter overview

This chapter explores:

- Motivation and emotion and their impact on student preparation for assessment
- Assessment myths which you may need to fight against
- Listening to students' voices about assessment

Introduction

The factors identified in Chapter 2 are unsettling in the context of the purposes of assessment which were discussed in Chapter 1. It is difficult to be sure that, for instance, an assessment is genuinely assessing the right amount and level of current knowledge, given the uncertainty we have introduced into thinking about the judgement process.

There are also some other considerations that can influence thinking about assessment, which we will look at in this chapter. Factors such as self-regulated learning, student motivation, emotional responses, and fixed beliefs are not always explicit in discussions about assessment, and they can stifle creative thinking about addressing the challenges we have already identified. Awareness of them is important when you are planning and carrying out assessment confidently in your own context.

Self-regulated learning

Self-regulated learning (Bandura, 1991) is an important concept in assessment, because it has been correlated with higher academic achievement (Zimmerman, 1990). According to Zimmerman, 'self-regulated learners plan, set goals, organize, self-monitor, and self-evaluate at various points during the process of acquisition' (1990, pp. 4–5). These behaviours can be learned, and you can build support for them into your assessment planning, so we will return to this concept regularly through Part 2 of the book.

Motivation and emotion

Assessment tends to generate strong feelings in both teachers and students. This is hardly surprising, when the purposes of assessment may include the achievement of a qualification which is important for beginning a career, or when considerable time and resources have been invested in an education which will be recognised and validated by the successful completion of an assessment task. The motivation to achieve academic success drives engagement with assessment and can lead to strong emotions: positive ones if the goal is achieved, and negative ones if it is not. The prospect of feeling these emotions also influences the student's preparation for assessment; a student can feel very driven by the desire to achieve their learning goals, but also overwhelmed by anxiety about failing. They may thus be able to spend a lot of time studying, but have difficulty in deciding what to focus on, so that they use that time less effectively.

The feeling most likely to come to mind when thinking about assessment is anxiety, and both teachers and students are likely to feel it. For students, 'test anxiety' is linked to unseen, time-constrained assessments such as written examinations, and is a well-studied concept in the psychology literature internationally (Hancock, 2001; Núñez-Peña et al., 2016; Rana & Mahmood, 2010) with an established inventory (Taylor & Deane, 2002). There are reported differences in test anxiety between male and female students (Núñez-Peña et al., 2016), and even between national systems (Lowe, 2019), and there is no shortage of strategies to try to reduce student anxiety (see, for instance, Rana & Mahmood, 2010, and many citing papers).

Student difficulties in engaging with assessment feedback have been linked to emotions (Paterson et al., 2020; Shields, 2015; Varlander, 2008), and motivation, emotion, and self-regulation were found to be interdependent in a large-scale study by Mega et al. (2014). More generalised anxiety around assessment is less well studied, although anecdotal examples are also easy enough to find. Think about your own experiences of being assessed in higher education. Did you ever feel anxious about the possible outcomes, or have uncertainty about what you were expected to do? However long ago it was, and however confident they are in their own abilities, most people can identify some periods during their education when they were anxious about an assessment. If you ask your students, it would be surprising if they didn't have stories of their own to tell, and their previous experiences will influence their approach to your assessment too.

You may come across colleagues who argue that a little stress can be very motivational; this has been found to be possible when the student feels some control over their ability to achieve, but not in an environment where there is uncertainty and the assessment is presented as being of very high **stakes** (Bonneville-Roussy et al., 2017). The 'right' amount of stress may be difficult to achieve. There are also studies which show that severe test anxiety is correlated with poorer motivation and assessment outcomes (Hancock, 2001; Núñez-Peña et al., 2016; Rana & Mahmood, 2010). Our list of the purposes of assessment in Table 1.2 did not include 'creating anxiety', and it makes sense to design assessment to aim to mitigate the inherent possibility of causing stress and to reinforce the idea that students can succeed in a particular assignment task. A teacher can do this by providing clear instructions for the assignment, discussing ways to plan and prepare for assessment, and scaffolding the final task with formative work so that the last steps provide a visible opportunity to bring together the work they have done during the course.

Staff anxiety around assessment is less well studied, although Myyry et al. (2019) reported feelings of stress around many of the uncertainties we considered in Chapter 2. Anecdotal evidence of staff anxiety about assessment is as easy to find as it is for students. In an informal study which simply involved asking new teachers how they felt about assessment, it was found that 70% used words linked to anxiety, such as 'stressful' and 'worrying' (Marr & Forsyth, 2010). It is reasonable to speculate about two major causes of teacher stress associated with assessment. First, uncertainty about standards of the kind we discussed in Chapter 2 can lead to anxiety about how well students are going to do in their final assessments – this can be a particular worry if the person who teaches the students is not the one completing the marking. It can also make the marking process more difficult, as it takes longer to make a grading decision and write feedback if one lacks confidence in the decision. The application of thoughtful assessment design techniques for all aspects of the assessment lifecycle should help with this uncertainty.

The second cause of teacher stress, which may be more significant for many, is pressure of workload and deadlines for marking. The capacity of the individual teacher to address this is more limited, although the selection of appropriate assignment tasks and efficient marking techniques can help with this. We will look at these in more detail in Chapter 6 and Part 3 of the book, respectively. Any underlying problem would need a collective discussion about workload, informed by careful reporting of the time actually taken to complete the marking.

Finally, it is important to remember the role of professional and administrative services teams in the management of assessment. They are usually responsible for auditing academic standards, managing student records, putting marks together for final qualifications, providing study support, having the right resources in the library, supporting the use of technical equipment in assessment, and collecting data on assessment. It is important to them that the process runs smoothly, reliably, and validly too, and they will have anxieties about getting their parts right. Find out who supports the different parts of the assessment lifecycle in your institution and build relationships with them so that everyone is aware of what you are doing and how it fits with the university processes.

Assessment myths

After working for many years as an academic developer in UK higher education, my practice has been strongly influenced by working with experienced, thoughtful colleagues who have shared with me some deeply-held beliefs about assessment in higher education that have turned out to have no basis in evidence or fact. These beliefs often postulate some kind of quasi-legal constraint on the design or management of assessment: perhaps about the size, or type, of assessment task which was allowed, whether group work could be fairly assessed, or how much information about assessment may be provided to students. Some regulatory frameworks may have rules about some of these matters, but the striking thing about these statements in general was that they tended to be presented as fact without further exploration.

It is to be expected that new members of staff are briefed about assessment by colleagues; this is of course an essential part of developing an effective teaching community that identifies and maintains academic standards. The potential pitfall is that deeply-held beliefs may be handed down from generation to generation of teachers without being questioned. As is so often the case with an oral tradition, the information may have taken on a mythical quality. Meanwhile, actual regulations may have changed without coming to the attention of all teachers, or the beliefs have become confused or embellished in the telling; students may now be coming to the course with a different set of previous qualifications or experiences, or the expectations of employers have been updated. A dependence on such myths may also mean that some of the factors outlined in Chapter 2, which definitely affect assessment, may have been relegated in importance compared to these apparent certainties.

In the UK, universities rely on the UK Quality Code (QAA, 2018) to develop their regulations. This code does not prescribe very much; it provides over-arching guidance which is then interpreted at institutional level. In general terms, it expects assessment to be aligned to learning outcomes and for there to be clear processes in place to manage procedures and practices, including some external oversight.

The Quality Code does not even specify a particular marking system. Although most UK universities use a percentage scale, some use a numerical score known as the Grade Point Average (GPA) and a couple use letter grades. Some universities may not even have the same scales in place for all programmes. The USA tends to use letter grades (A–F, where F is a fail) which can be converted to a GPA. In Australia, the exact grading system is dependent on the state, but is letter based. German universities grade from 1–5, where 1 is the best mark, French teachers mark out of 20 where 20 is the highest grade, and Swedish universities use a variety of approaches. Across the European Union, qualifications are considered to be equivalent despite the variety of grading systems, and bachelor's degrees are generally recognised by employers in different countries to demonstrate similar standards, so it is reasonable to assume that the marking scales are not very important in themselves. You will need to fit in with institutional or departmental norms, but you could challenge anyone who suggests that 'their' way is based in evidence or even common practice.

While there is no national expectation about assignment size, some UK universities have 'tariffs' for the size of an assignment task, specifying how many words a particular type of assignment should have, for instance. Others may only permit the use of certain types of task, or have rules (real or imagined) about marking criteria or feedback. Such rules are likely to be quite generic and open to interpretation, so you may be able to be creative if it suits your assignment design.

Somewhere in your university there will be a single source of truth on these matters, probably in the form of an assessment framework and regulations, and I strongly recommend that you track down the relevant documentation before you begin any serious work in developing your own assessment plans. If you are in a different country and want to check the requirements nationally, the website of your national quality agency will have the details. I haven't seen any yet, but I would be interested to know if you do discover a national tariff of assignment sizes, and I will then accept that it may not be a myth everywhere.

If you teach on a course which is regulated by an external body, it is also essential to find out more about their actual requirements. It is often said, for instance, that a professional body will not approve a course without it being assessed by a set of unseen, timed examinations, but their documentation may not actually say this when you look at it. External bodies that provide accreditation will employ an education or assessments officer or team, who will usually be prepared to discuss assessment methods with those who are designing courses.

Creating a shared understanding of assessment across a discipline and a team is very important in the development of a coherent higher education course. As part of these conversations, it is important for you and your colleagues to consider the possibility that you may have internalised some assessment myths. False certainties about the rules can be pervasive and persistent, and can have a lingering effect on innovation in assessment. If everyone around you believes that essays are the only permitted way to assess the students on your programme, then you will find it difficult to make headway with your radical proposal to replace one essay with a work-based project. If you want to bring about change in that situation, you will need to engage in some myth-busting. You may need to identify allies in educational development (a centre for learning and teaching, or similar), in the academic registry or the department responsible for regulatory frameworks, or with your professional bodies. Particularly when working with people outside your immediate department or disciplinary area, you may find it useful to avoid formulations such as, 'Am I allowed to replace an essay with a work-based project?' and frame your enquiry as, 'We would like to introduce a work-based project to provide a more authentic assessment opportunity for our students. What is the process for making this change?'

Students' voices in assessment management

The last element to add in here brings together the two preceding sections. If assessment is making many of us anxious, and we accept the proposition that it is possible to change assessment, then it makes sense to discuss improvements with all stakeholders. We have already touched on the need to talk to professional bodies, to employers, and to members of the university administration about changes to assessment, but what about students?

Collecting student views formally can look like an industrial activity. In many countries and institutions, students are frequently surveyed to find out their opinions of their higher education. There is a variety of standardised national instruments, such as the UK's National Student Survey (NSS), the National Survey of Student Engagement (NSSE) in the USA, the Australasian Survey of Student Experience (AuSSE), and South Africa's Survey of Student Engagement (SASSE).

The questions in these national surveys are quite general, looking at overall experiences, rather than giving you feedback on your own teaching and assessment, and they are intended to show trends and comparisons between institutions, rather than as a direct enhancement tool. All of these surveys ask questions which are useful in relation to assessment, so you can use them to identify some general points about students' perceptions of whether assessment is fair (NSS), or whether they engaged in synthesising and organising ideas, information, or experiences into new, more complex interpretations and relationships (AuSSE), or were involved in practices which are considered to have a high impact on learning (SASSE).

It is common, if not ubiquitous, for individual universities also to survey their students to find out their opinions of courses and modules. Your university may have a standardised survey, or you may send out surveys which are tailored to your department or course. You should be able to ask for more information from the course leader, director of studies, or head of department or school (as appropriate) in your institution.

Assessment audits are a useful way to review practices across a course, and should include students' voices in the process. In the UK, the Transforming the Experience of Students through Assessment (TESTA) methodology has been developed (Jessop et al., 2014) to take a holistic look at course assessment practices and effectiveness. In this approach, there are three main elements: a review of course documentation and mapping of the types of assessment a student is expected to complete; a student questionnaire looking at students' experiences of assessment on the course; and focus groups with students near the end of the course. A review of these elements enables a course team to look at consistency of approach across all individual modules and to consider the role of individual assignments in contributing to the overall goals of the qualification. Many resources to support the design of 'Programme-Focused Assessment' (Whitfield & Hartley, 2019) were developed at the University of Bradford and are freely available on the internet. Taking a course-level overview may be difficult for you if you are only responsible for one module, or part, or a course, but it is a valuable exercise to undertake with colleagues, perhaps when a programme is being reviewed or rewritten.

Students' experiences of assessment have been a focus of much useful research into different parts of the lifecycle, covering topics such as receiving and processing feedback (Chanock, 2000; Shields, 2015), and the use of different types of tasks and activity: for example, group work (Bramley, 2019; Hannaford, 2016; Moore & Hampton, 2015). We will return to specific areas of this literature in Part 2, when we consider the design of assignment tasks.

If you want to find out more about your own students' views on your assessment tasks, you can take a more personalised approach. You won't be trying to compare with other courses or universities, but to identify what is working, or not. To find out how things are going during a module, you can ask quick questions as part of a teaching session, using the one-minute paper technique where you ask all students a single, short question (Stead, 2005). This is a good way to find out how prepared students feel, or if there is anything in the assignment brief they don't understand, or what they plan to do with their feedback.

You may be considering a more substantial change in an assignment task. In many universities, this would need to be planned for the following year or cohort, as it is difficult to change the details of tasks once they have been published to students. This means that your plans might not affect the current students, which could affect their willingness to participate. However, you could start with a simple survey to all students. You could include questions about assessment which would help you to judge the effectiveness of different elements of your assessment activity. These questions could be quite open, asking them about their feelings about assessment and what they might do to change it, or you could ask them what they think of a proposed change. Table 3.1 has some examples. Note that it wouldn't be recommended to ask all of these at once.

The questions you choose to ask will depend on the type of assignment and your knowledge of your students. They are just some ideas to help your thinking.

Table 3.1 Sample questions for students when considering an assessment change

- What's the best assignment you've ever been set, and what did you like about it?
- What kinds of assignment motivate you to give your best? (You could add examples of assignment types if you like, especially if you are considering something new.)
- If you could design your own assignment for this module, what would it be like?
- From your previous experiences, what are the pros and cons of group assessments?
- What's the most useful piece of feedback on your academic work that you have ever received?
- What kinds of feedback would you like to receive on your academic work?

Questions about students' ability to self-regulate (to help you decide whether to include strategies explicitly to support this):

- How soon after the beginning of the module do you start on the assignment?
- What do you do to get yourself started on your assignment?
- Do you ever review your final drafts in relation to the marking criteria, to check that you've covered everything?
- What's your most successful strategy for finding resources from the library or elsewhere?
- To help me plan the right support for the group, can you rate your current skills in relation to assessment preparation? Use a scale of 1–5, where 1 is very easy, and 5 is very difficult.
  In relation to assessment preparation, I find it easy to:
  - Plan my time
  - Set goals
  - Organise my work
  - Evaluate how well I'm doing
  - Estimate my final grade

Think carefully about what you will do with the survey outcomes. Brooman et al. (2014) describe a chastening experience of carrying out a module redesign based on a questionnaire about the existing structure, but without asking students about the proposals developed in response to the survey. In their second attempt, they used focus groups to explore their proposals with students, and ended up with a course design which was much more successful.

If you want to involve students more actively, you could involve a group of them in redesigning the assessment task. As in the previous paragraph, this is unlikely to have an impact on the students who are involved. They may be motivated to improve assessment for a future cohort, but their engagement might be limited if they will not see any benefit themselves. In some universities, students might be able to gain credits, or be paid, for such an activity, which might help motivation.

The concept of involving students in co-creating their own curriculum and assessments could be taken a stage further by allowing them to design aspects of their own assessment tasks to demonstrate achievement of the learning outcomes for the module. In this situation, they would be having a direct influence on their own assessments and not those of future students. Deeley and Bovill (2015) provide a detailed case study which evaluates the student response to a range of different co-creation ideas in assessment at postgraduate level.

In some disciplinary areas, this may seem like quite a leap from current practice, but in others, it is already commonplace. In the last years of study in art and design, for instance, it would be normal for students to negotiate the form of their output. However, if the usual assessment is an unseen mathematical examination for first-year accountancy students, you might struggle to see the possibilities of student involvement in task design. As ever, there is a range of possible interventions that could be made: students could be involved in writing questions for an exam, you could discuss appropriate marking criteria with them, you could ask them what kind of feedback they would find useful for a particular task, and so on. We will return to this idea when we look at individual types of assignment task in Part 3.

Conclusion

This chapter has explored some issues which don't necessarily get much explicit attention, but which may affect assessment practices. Being aware of the possible impact of these factors is important when you are making decisions about your own assessments.

Further reading

If you'd like to develop your thinking about student involvement in assessment further, then Falchikov (2013) has a lot of ideas.

A more recent guide was produced by Advance HE in the UK (Bovill et al., 2021).

Ajjawi et al. (2021) looks at the strategies students use to progress after failing an aspect of their academic work; it can be useful to think about what works as well as what doesn't.

References

Ajjawi, R., Dracup, M., & Boud, D. (2021). Hero, survivor or stuck: A narrative analysis of student constructions of persistence after failure. *Teaching in Higher Education*, https://doi.org/10.1080/13562517.2021.1952569

Bandura, A. (1991). Social cognitive theory of self-regulation. *Organizational Behavior and Human Decision Processes*, *50*(2), 248–287. https://doi.org/https://doi.org/10.1016/0749-5978(91)90022-L

Bonneville-Roussy, A., Evans, P., Verner-Filion, J., Vallerand, R. J., & Bouffard, T. (2017). Motivation and coping with the stress of assessment: Gender differences in outcomes for university students. *Contemporary Educational Psychology*, *48*, 28–42. https://doi.org/https://doi.org/10.1016/j.cedpsych.2016.08.003

Bovill, C., Matthews, K., & Hinchcliffe, T. (2021). *Student Partnerships in Assessment (SPiA)*. Oxford: Advance HE. www.advance-he.ac.uk/knowledge-hub/student-partnerships-assessment-spia

Bramley, G. (2019). There is no 'I' in 'a team of lawyers': An evaluation of student perceptions of group assessment within legal higher education. *The Law Teacher*, 1–14. https://doi.org/10.1080/03069400.2019.1582279

Brooman, S., Darwent, S., & Pimor, A. (2014). The student voice in higher education curriculum design: Is there value in listening? *Innovations in Education and Teaching International*, 1–12. https://doi.org/10.1080/14703297.2014.910128

Chanock, K. (2000). Comments on Essays: Do students understand what tutors write? *Teaching in Higher Education*, 5(1), 95–105. http://dx.doi.org/10.1080/135625100114984

Deeley, S. J., & Bovill, C. (2015). Staff student partnership in assessment: Enhancing assessment literacy through democratic practices. *Assessment & Evaluation in Higher Education*, 1–15. https://doi.org/10.1080/02602938.2015.1126551

Falchikov, N. (2013). *Improving assessment through student involvement: Practical solutions for aiding learning in higher and further education*. London: Routledge.

Hancock, D. R. (2001). Effects of test anxiety and evaluative threat on students' achievement and motivation. *The Journal of educational research*, 94(5), 284–290.

Hannaford, L. (2016). Motivation in group assessment: A phenomenological approach to post-graduate group assessment. *Assessment & Evaluation in Higher Education*, 1–14. https://doi.org/10.1080/02602938.2016.1195787

Jessop, T., El Hakim, Y., & Gibbs, G. (2014). The whole is greater than the sum of its parts: A large-scale study of students' learning in response to different programme assessment patterns. *Assessment & Evaluation in Higher Education*, 39(1), 73–88. https://doi.org/10.1080/02602938.2013.792108

Lowe, P. A. (2019). Cross-national comparison between UK and US Higher Education students in test anxiety. *Higher Education Studies*, 9(3), 88–97.

Marr, L., & Forsyth, R. (2010). *Identity crisis: Working in HE in the 21st century*. Stoke-on-Trent: Trentham Books.

Mega, C., Ronconi, L., & De Beni, R. (2014). What makes a good student? How emotions, self-regulated learning, and motivation contribute to academic achievement. *Journal of Educational Psychology*, 106(1), 121–131. https://doi.org/10.1037/a0033546

Moore, P., & Hampton, G. (2015). 'It's a bit of a generalisation, but …': Participant perspectives on intercultural group assessment in higher education. *Assessment & Evaluation in Higher Education*, 40(3), 390–406. https://doi.org/10.1080/02602938.2014.919437

Myyry, L., Karaharju-Suvanto, T., Vesalainen, M., Virtala, A.-M., Raekallio, M., Salminen, O., Vuorensola, K., & Nevgi, A. (2019). Experienced academics' emotions related to assessment. *Assessment & Evaluation in Higher Education*, 1–13. https://doi.org/10.1080/02602938.2019.1601158

Núñez-Peña, M. I., Suárez-Pellicioni, M., & Bono, R. (2016). Gender differences in test anxiety and their impact on higher education students' academic achievement. *Procedia-Social and Behavioral Sciences*, 228, 154–160.

Paterson, C., Paterson, N., Jackson, W., & Work, F. (2020). What are students' needs and preferences for academic feedback in higher education? A systematic review. *Nurse Education Today*, 85, 104236. https://doi.org/https://doi.org/10.1016/j.nedt.2019.104236

QAA. (2018). *The revised UK Quality Code for Higher Education*. London: Quality Assurance Agency for Higher Education. www.qaa.ac.uk/quality-code

Rana, R., & Mahmood, N. (2010). The relationship between test anxiety and academic achievement. *Bulletin of Education and research*, 32(2), 63–74.

Shields, S. (2015). 'My work is bleeding': Exploring students' emotional responses to first-year assignment feedback. *Teaching in Higher Education*, 20(6), 614–624. https://doi.org/10.1080/13562517.2015.1052786

Stead, D. R. (2005). A review of the one-minute paper. *Active Learning in Higher Education*, *6*(2), 118–131. http://alh.sagepub.com/cgi/content/abstract/6/2/118

Taylor, J., & Deane, F. P. (2002). Development of a short form of the Test Anxiety Inventory (TAI). *The Journal of General Psychology*, *129*(2), 127–136.

Varlander, S. (2008). The role of students' emotions in formal feedback situations. *Teaching in Higher Education*, *13*(2), 145–156. www.informaworld.com/10.1080/13562510801923195

Whitfield, R., & Hartley, P. (2019). Assessment strategy: Enhancement of student learning through a programme focus. In A. Diver (Ed.), *Employability via Higher Education: Sustainability as scholarship* (pp. 237–253). Cham, CH: Springer International. https://doi.org/10.1007/978-3-030-26342-3_16

Zimmerman, B. J. (1990). Self-regulated learning and academic achievement: An overview. *Educational Psychologist*, *25*(1), 3–17. https://doi.org/10.1207/s15326985ep2501_2

4

ASSESSMENT IN THE CONTEMPORARY UNIVERSITY

Chapter overview

This chapter explores:

- The ways in which tradition and convention may impede creative thinking
- Differences between subject disciplines
- Grade inflation

Introduction

So far, we have looked at factors which might affect assessment design and management that are mainly internal to the university: how you and your colleagues think about assessment, the regulatory framework, students' expectations and reactions, and the relationships between assessment and the purposes of learning. In this chapter we will start to explore some of the external influences on assessment and think about how they impact on your decision-making.

The influence of tradition

In Chapter 1, we talked about what assessment in higher education is for; we didn't question the purpose of universities themselves. But of course, the vision and values projected by an individual institution may be reflected in the design and management of assignment tasks. For centuries, universities worldwide were fairly homogeneous in their approach to teaching and assessment: there were lectures (a legacy of the times when books and reading skills were scarce, and the lecturer (reader) was the single conduit to new knowledge), and examinations to test men's recall of the contents of the readings, and later on, to analyse and comment on them. In the UK, higher education was an optional activity for those who would inherit land and titles, but an essential preparation for those who needed a profession, such as becoming a minister of the church. In the nineteenth century, it became a pathway to the safe career of becoming a senior colonial administrator, as well as developing importance for professions such as law and medicine, and new civic universities were founded by wealthy businessmen as a contribution to the community. Universities also began to house important scientific laboratories, and the values of critical analysis and the creation of new knowledge started to become more important than recall.

During the same period, formal education developed in other ways too. Schooling began to be compulsory in many countries, and the age at which students completed this obligatory phase gradually increased. Education for other professions, such as nursing, teaching, accountancy, engineering, and domestic sciences, also became more formalised in technical colleges and apprentices began to be released to these institutions part-time to complement their professional development. These developments set the scene for the later expansion of higher education.

As the twentieth century dawned, women began to be allowed to attend universities, if not to take final assessments. The qualifications available for the 'technical' professions became more advanced and over the last few decades of the twentieth century and the beginning of the twenty-first, were initially aligned to undergraduate qualifications and then widely developed into bachelor's degrees in their own right. Alongside these changes in relation to the range, purpose, and value of undergraduate awards, attitudes to participation in higher education have evolved considerably, so that universities are now accessible to many more people. In 1950, 3.4% of 17–30 year-olds in the UK attended university (Bolton, 2012); in 2015, the number was 48% (HE Analysis Team, 2016). This increase in rates of participation happened earlier in the US (during the 1960s), as noted by Becher and Trowler (2001), citing Trow (1972).

These changes in participation in higher education are important to this discussion because universities, like all institutions, are affected by their history. 'The way that we do things around here' is passed from one generation of teachers to the next. The assumptions and intentions of the civic-minded sponsors of 'new' nineteenth-century universities, or the liberal goals of expansion of provision in the 1960s and 1990s, still have an impact on the ways that staff in the successors of these institutions teach and assess students.

It's easy to drop into stereotypes: perhaps we think about universities that have been around for centuries as tending to retain many traditional forms of assessment, such as unseen examinations and essays, while universities that started their existence as technical or community colleges may be thought to remain more comfortable with practical examinations. These stereotypes can and do extend into thinking about whether assessments in different universities are comparable with each other, and whether an increase in participation is necessarily linked to a reduction in academic standards and what is commonly known as grade inflation (Bachan, 2015). From the discussion in Chapter 2, you will be aware that there are many factors that influence the award of individual grades, which may make simple judgements about grade validity difficult to support. However, there is sustained evidence of increases in grades in UK universities (Bachan, 2015; Elton, 1998; Wyse et al., 2020). The UK parliament carried out an enquiry into the phenomenon in 2008 which attracted plenty of strongly-worded evidence submissions (IUSS, 2009), and you will readily find articles in national newspapers in many countries which bemoan the perceived negative link between graduate standards and the increase in the number of universities.

Leaving the stereotypes aside, discussion about grade inflation is not just about academic snobbery and the notion that one university is better than another. Elton (1998) found evidence for systematic grade inflation in what he called the 'old' universities in the UK between 1972 and 1992; he linked it not to massification of higher education, but to changes in the use of assessment tasks, with a move away from unseen, timed examinations to coursework.

Sadler (2009) points out that the integrity of grades matters to many people: to students, who will be motivated to achieve if they believe the grades have meaning; to the universities themselves, which will make decisions about progression between levels; to external monitors of quality (these are usually quasi-governmental bodies, in most countries) which must decide whether a university can continue to take students and how much education should be funded; and to future employers or researchers who wish to employ the students.

The influence of discipline

Generalisations about the type of university are simplistic, and don't take account of the wide range of subjects taught in a modern university. As well as institutional differences, it is commonly held that different parts of a university express their visions of assessment in very different ways, particularly in relation to individual subject areas. There have been some attempts to create taxonomies of difference between disciplines in order to provide structure to this kind of discussion. Notably, Becher (1994) built on the work of Biglan (1973), which categorised disciplines against different dimensions, to propose four categories of academic discipline: hard pure (natural sciences), hard applied (science-based professions), soft pure (humanities and social sciences), and soft applied (education and social professions). These groupings have been very influential in higher education studies and have survived into contemporary classifications (Simpson, 2017).

Both Biglan and Becher focused on the aims of research work when they were considering difference in these disciplinary areas, rather than on the approaches taken by specialists in the field of teaching and assessment. Becher and Trowler (2001, p. 196) consider some of the possible impact on teaching and assessment, and Neumann et al. (2002) take this a little further, but the work is largely theoretical. As part of the TESTA methodology (Jessop et al., 2014) we mentioned in Chapter 3, Jessop and Maleckar (2016, p. 169) have used audits of assessment to map assignment types to these disciplinary groups, as shown in Table 4.1.

Table 4.1 Types of assessment by discipline group

Discipline group	Assessment emphasis	Types of assessment used
'Hard pure'	Memorisation; application of course content; fact retention; and solving logical problems	Examinations; practical work; laboratory reports; numeric calculations; and multiple-choice quiz
'Hard applied'	Practical competence; application of theory to practice; and factual understanding	Multiple-choice quiz; examinations; simulations; and case studies
'Soft pure'	Analysis and synthesis of course content; and continuous assessment	Essays; oral presentations; short-answer papers; and project reports
'Soft applied'	Emphasis on personal growth and intellectual breadth; and application of theory to practice	Simulation; and case studies

You might be able to compare this with your own experiences of assessment. An art school which regards itself as avant-garde may want its students to show their independence and quirkiness in unconventional exhibitions – I have happy memories of visiting a pop-up 1940s tearoom which was run for a week by students from a School of Art as their group project, complete with scavenged china and birdcages, and individually-designed uniforms. I assume that they passed the assignment, although I have no idea how it might have been graded. A mechanical engineering department might specialise in automotive design and require students to learn how to design engine parts which are tested in a real vehicle, whereas another down the road might focus on factory processes. An economics team may pride itself on the rigour of its unseen examinations. Healthcare disciplines may have quite tightly prescribed assessments based on practical tests, possibly set by external bodies. All of these are valid assessments.

The influence of individual experiences and expectations

Both institutional and disciplinary history are likely to affect decision-making about assess-ment. To this, you can add the expectations of individual teachers. Staff in the contem-porary university may have had very diverse assessment experiences from one another, even though they now work in the same department. They may have studied in differ-ent countries, or in different 'types' of university, using the clumsy stereotypes previously mentioned, or worked in industries or professions where particular assessment types have shown themselves to be especially valuable. The discussions from Chapter 2 will also have shown you that individual views about assessment, including your own tacit knowledge, are likely to be very powerful.

At the national level, the organisations that provide external monitoring of quality (see Weber et al., 2010, for a short comparison of some of these bodies) may try to set some threshold standards or expectations, such as *The Frameworks for Higher Education Qualifications of UK Degree-Awarding Bodies* (QAA, 2014) in the UK. These expectations will then be interpreted at institution and disciplinary levels. Becher (1994) categorises discussions about higher education systems, institutions, and at the departmental level as macro, meso, and micro, respectively. You may not need to find out in great detail about what's happening at these three levels. This book is aimed more at individuals and your own agency in designing and managing assessment, and the purpose of this chapter is to make you aware of the influences at the other three levels, so that you can take them into account when taking your own decisions about assessment.

There is a growing literature which aims to increase assessment literacy and improve the quality of decision-making about assessment. Making choices about assessment is work that happens most usefully in course and module teams, and we will focus on the module level as we set out practical steps for each stage of the assessment lifecycle in Part 2 of the book.

Conclusion

Detailed decisions about assessment design and management need to be made at the level of the course and the individual modules, but it is important to be aware of the context in which those decisions are made. In Part 1 we have covered the basic principles of assessment, the challenges presented by validity, fairness, and reliability, and the need to listen carefully to what students, colleagues, and external stakeholders have to say about assessment. The key message to take forward is that you are not obliged to reproduce traditional assessment patterns, but you do need to use a range of information to make and support your decisions.

Further reading

This report from the UK professional body for higher education teaching, Advance HE, which was previously known as the Higher Education Academy, gives a good overview of the challenges to be addressed in making changes to assessment (Various authors, 2012).

References

Bachan, R. (2015). Grade inflation in UK higher education. *Studies in Higher Education*, 1–21. https://doi.org/10.1080/03075079.2015.1019450

Becher, T. (1994). The significance of disciplinary differences. *Studies in Higher Education*, *19*(2), 151–161.

Becher, T., & Trowler, P. R. (2001). *Academic tribes and territories* (2nd ed.). Buckingham: Open University Press/SRHE.

Biglan, A. (1973). The characteristics of subject matter in different academic areas. *Journal of Applied Psychology*, *57*(3), 195–203. https://doi.org/10.1037/h0034701

Bolton, P. (2012). *Education: Historical statistics*. London: House of Commons.

Elton, L. (1998). Are UK degree standards going up, down or sideways? *Studies in Higher Education*, *23*(1), 35–42. http://dx.doi.org/10.1080/03075079812331380472

HE Analysis Team. (2016). *Participation rates in higher education: Academic years 2006/2007 – 2014/2015 (Provisional)*. London: UK Government. Retrieved from www.gov.uk/government/uploads/system/uploads/attachment_data/file/552886/HEIPR_PUBLICATION_2014-15.pdf

IUSS. (2009). *Students and universities*. Innovation, Universities, Science and Skills Committee Reports. London: UK Parliament. www.publications.parliament.uk/pa/cm/cmdius.htm

Jephcote, C., Medland, E., & Lygo-Baker, S. (2021). Grade inflation versus grade improvement: Are our students getting more intelligent? *Assessment & Evaluation in Higher Education*, *46*(4), 547–571. https://doi.org/10.1080/02602938.2020.1795617

Jessop, T., El Hakim, Y., & Gibbs, G. (2014). The whole is greater than the sum of its parts: A large-scale study of students' learning in response to different programme assessment patterns. *Assessment & Evaluation in Higher Education*, *39*(1), 73–88. https://doi.org/10.1080/02602938.2013.792108

Jessop, T., & Maleckar, B. (2016). The influence of disciplinary assessment patterns on student learning: A comparative study. *Studies in Higher Education*, *41*(4), 696–711. https://doi.org/10.1080/03075079.2014.943170

Neumann, R., Parry, S., & Becher, T. (2002). Teaching and learning in their disciplinary contexts: A conceptual analysis. *Studies in Higher Education, 27*(4), 405–417.

Norton, L., Floyd, S., & Norton, B. (2019). Lecturers' views of assessment design, marking and feedback in higher education: A case for professionalisation? *Assessment & Evaluation in Higher Education*, 1–13. https://doi.org/10.1080/02602938.2019.1592110

QAA. (2014). *The frameworks for higher education qualifications of UK degree-awarding bodies.* London: Quality Assurance Agency for Higher Education. www.qaa.ac.uk/docs/qaa/quality-code/qualifications-frameworks.pdf

Sadler, D. R. (2009). Grade integrity and the representation of academic achievement. *Studies in Higher Education, 34*(7), 807–826. www.informaworld.com/10.1080/03075070802706553

Simpson, A. (2017). The surprising persistence of Biglan's classification scheme. *Studies in Higher Education, 42*(8), 1520–1531.

Trow, M. (1972). The expansion and transformation of higher education. *International Review of Education, 18*, 61–84.

Various authors. (2012). *A Marked Improvement: Transforming assessment in higher education.* Oxford: Advance HE. https://www.advance-he.ac.uk/knowledge-hub/marked-improvement-transforming-assessment-higher-education-assessment-review-tool

Weber, L., Mahfooz, S. B., & Hovde, K. (2010). *Quality assurance in higher education: A comparison of eight systems.* Washington, DC: World Bank.

Wyse, S., Page, B., Walkington, H., & Hill, J. L. (2020). Degree outcomes and national calibration: Debating academic standards in UK Geography. *Area, 52*(2), 376–385. https://doi.org/https://doi.org/10.1111/area.12571

PART 2

MAKING
ASSESSMENT WORK

In Part 1 of the book, we set out the purposes of assessment in higher education and introduced many of the challenges which you may encounter when trying to design fair, valid, and reliable assessment. In Part 2, we will show how you can address these challenges and develop a confident approach to assessment design and management. Each chapter takes you through the process of planning a part of the assessment lifecycle.

5

DESIGNING EFFECTIVE ASSESSMENT TASKS

Chapter overview

This chapter explores:

- Confident approaches to assessment design
- Choosing an assignment task
- Authenticity and equity in assessment design

Introduction

This chapter focuses on the selection and configuration of the assignment task, with consideration of the choices you will make in designing inclusive, accessible, and authentic assessment which is relevant to contemporary society and future employment.

Key questions

Designing an assignment task is part of the first point on the assessment lifecycle: setting (Figure 1.4). As a rule of thumb, your new task should show that students have achieved the module learning outcomes, be straightforward to mark, and be understandable to students. It is also a reasonable aspiration to design something that you would actually enjoy marking. In their submissions, students are showing how well they have understood what they have been taught, and synthesising their learning into an original piece of work in your own subject area. We have already suggested that marking can feel stressful, because of the constraints of time, and the difficulty of making precise judgements about student work, but seeing the students' work should be something a teacher looks forward to.

This gives you four questions you can ask about any assignment task:

1   Validity: Does it let students demonstrate achievement of the learning outcomes?
2   Manageability: Will it be straightforward to mark, give feedback, and moderate?
3   Clarity: Will students understand what to do and see how this task fits into their course overall?
4   Satisfaction: Will I look forward to marking it?

You could also add a fifth factor: will the students enjoy doing it? That is more difficult for the teacher to control, so this hasn't been added to the core questions, but it is certainly worth suggesting to students that assignments can be enjoyable, and asking them after completion what they have got out of the process.

The question of validity has an important secondary question about accessibility and inclusive design: will all students have an equal opportunity to demonstrate their achievement? Nieminen (2022) proposes five principles for ensuring inclusive assessment: rethinking accommodations, anti-ableist work, celebration of human diversity, student partnership, and interdependence. I would replace 'anti-ableist' with 'anti-discriminatory', to broaden the scope of thinking, but these are all key principles for inclusion. The assumption should be that all assessments are accessible to all students as they are designed. Of course, there will sometimes be exceptions: students with unexpected circumstances which affect their ability to complete a task, or a requirement from an external body which can't be changed, but in general, the presumption should be that all students accepted onto a programme should be able to attempt all the assignment tasks without special adjustments or accommodations. In order to model this expectation, I presume that all aspects of assessment design and management are intended to be inclusive, so discussion of inclusive practice is integrated in the following sections rather than covered as a separate topic. The explanations of different types of assignment task in Part 3 include discussion of inclusive practice.

Key decisions

Assignment briefs

The description of an assignment task is often called an assignment brief. If this is the first time you have written an assignment brief, then the process outlined here will step you through it. It will be useful to have examples of briefs from other modules on your course available for comparison.

The information you are expected to include may be prescribed by your university, and thus will vary from place to place, but Table 5.1 provides a fairly typical list. This is probably sufficient to develop a brief. It is easy to add too much information and cause confusion, even if it is trying to explain things in a different way. Try to stick to a simple description which relates clearly to the learning outcomes, otherwise it may look to the students as through there are two sets of requirements.

Table 5.1   Key information for an assignment brief

Weighting of the task, as a percentage of the total credits for the module	If the module has more than one task, then say what percentage of the module assessment this task represents.
Module learning outcomes which are covered by the task	For a module with a single task, this will be all of them, but if the module has more than one task, you should indicate which learning outcomes are covered.
Assessment method	This would be a one- or two-word description of the task (such as essay, examination, presentation).
Submission size	This should provide an indication of the size of the submission you expect from students, such as a 2,000-word essay or a 10-minute presentation.
Timing	When the assignment(s) will be submitted during the module.
Description	A short explanation of what students are expected to do, including the expected size of the assignment task and any particular requirements, e.g. group work, special submission techniques or specialist resources needed. A peer reviewer or a student should have a clear sense of what is expected from reading this description.
Feedback strategy	Outline what kind of feedback you will provide, and what you expect students to do with it.
Formative support	Explain what support is available to students as they prepare their assignments. This could be specific tasks which will help them prepare, information about your availability to students, and/or signposting to university services.

I am sure it is obvious that the brief needs to be written in student-friendly language. Scull (2001) found that students presented with a selection of similarly structured assignment briefs generally found them easy to understand, but often found that the briefs contained jargon which confused them. We all use specialist terms. Asking a current student or a colleague from a slightly different discipline to review your briefs and highlight words which need further explanation should ensure that your briefs are jargon-free. Using a similar structure in all modules of the course will also help students to locate the information they need with confidence.

Assessment method
Coursework or examination?

The type of assignment is probably the first thing you will think about. The first decision you need to make is whether to make the task time-constrained, which we will refer to as an examination, or completed over a period of time, which we will refer to as coursework. This will narrow down the choice of tasks, although of course there are plenty of tasks, such as an essay, which can be designed to be completed under time constraint or over a longer period. Table 5.2 lists some generic tasks which are explored in detail in Part 3.

Table 5.2   Generic assessment types

Coursework: Not time-constrained	Examination: Time-constrained
Article	Unseen examination – open-book
Bibliography	Seen examination
Biography	Take-home examination
Blog	Open-book examination
Case study	Objective structured (clinical) examination (OSCE)
Competence portfolio	Practical examination
Event	Multiple-choice test
Essay	Oral examination
Poster	Performance or show
Synthesis portfolio or patchwork text	Presentation

This initial decision to choose between examination and coursework is important because they test different types of learning outcomes. Examinations test recall and ability to work under pressure of time, providing a snapshot of student performance; coursework allows ideas to be developed over time, discussed, and refined. Most higher education programmes will ask students to complete both types of work, reflecting the different situations they may face in future employment or educational contexts. It is worth noting that time-constrained examinations have been linked to higher levels of assessment anxiety and students with particular disabilities (particularly specific learning disabilities such as dyslexia, but also certain mental health conditions) may find long, written examinations particularly difficult.

Perhaps the decision about whether or not the task is time-constrained is made for you, due to institutional customs or structures, or the requirements of your professional body, but if you would like to do something different, it is always worth checking to see if there is any flexibility in their approach. Sometimes, things are how they are because that's how they've always been.

Type of task

You may already have an idea in mind, or you may be planning to use something you've done before. Part 3 of the book lists different types of assignment with commentary on their use. Before you reach for the most familiar option, you could have a browse through the examples and see if they spark ideas for trying something new.

First, consider whether the task will address one or more of your module learning outcomes. If there is only one task for the whole module, then of course it needs to cover all of the outcomes. There is no good evidence either way as to whether it is better to have multiple summative tasks rather than a single large task for a module. The argument for multiple tasks is that it reduces the pressure on students, as they can complete several 'low stakes' tasks and accumulate grades more gently. On the other hand, it may be difficult for them to develop sustained thinking about the topic. This approach also creates more administration for the teacher, which is a significant consideration with large classes.

Single assignment tasks are higher stakes to the student, which may create anxiety, but they do allow them to tackle a subject in more depth. The anxiety can be mitigated by including formative assessment and supporting the development of the assignment during teaching. We will return to strategies for scaffolding student preparation for assessment in Chapter 6.

Table 5.3 takes the sample learning outcomes from Chapter 1 and suggests tasks which might be suitable. These are only suggestions; there will almost always be a choice of tasks which will work equally well to demonstrate achievement of the learning outcomes. You can create a shortlist, and then move on to the other three factors: manageability, clarity, and satisfaction.

We have already considered some of the reasons why it may feel safer to stick with traditional forms of assessment, but there really is no evidence to show that the type of assessment has a negative impact on academic standards or on student performance. In making a choice, you may find it more useful to think about the four key questions of validity, manageability, clarity, and satisfaction. Manageability may be a strong factor: is it possible for you to set up and grade a particular type of assessment with the time and resources available to you?

Table 5.3 Learning outcomes and assessment tasks

Learning outcome	Suitable tasks
Define the basic concepts of [a specific topic in the subject area]	• Unseen examination / Multiple-choice test Note: I wouldn't recommend coursework for this kind of learning outcome; you will simply receive almost identical lists from every student, which will be uninteresting to mark and easy to produce without much thought. It might be necessary if students must master this knowledge to proceed to more analytical work, but it is worth questioning the value of such a learning outcome before you proceed to assessment design.
Summarise literature from [a specific topic in the subject area]	• Annotated bibliography, relating each reading to the course directly • Literature review, linking the readings together
Explain the differences between [different schools of thought in the subject area]	• Essay • Debate • Presentation • Poster
Critically analyse results of experiments undertaken to investigate [a specific topic in the subject area]	• Laboratory report (if own experiments) • Essay (if reviewing other people's work) • Article for popular press • Poster • Presentation
Evaluate the effect of [a specific topic in the subject area] on [a generic topic in the subject area]	• Essay • Scientific article • Debate

Making a more creative choice may enable you to match the task more closely to your intended learning outcomes, or consider outcomes that are more focused on professional or thematic work. For instance, an adaptation might make it easier to bring the UN Sustainability Goals into your subject, or to replicate an activity that a student may encounter in a future workplace. The use of 'authentic' tasks in assessment is another factor which is thought to improve student engagement and help them to prepare for the world after higher education. In a comprehensive review of the use of authentic assessment, Villarroel et al. (2018) developed a definition and suggested that an assessment task which is authentic needs to be set in a realistic and rich context, to represent a worthwhile task, perhaps involving external stakeholders, and requiring higher-order skills to complete it.

Some assignment tasks may also make it easier for you to give students the opportunity to show what they are bringing to their course in addition to what you are teaching them. A case study about small businesses might be enhanced by asking them to use their experiences of paid work, for instance; an essay on a historical period could invite some reflection from the perspective of different cultures rather than the one dominant in your own country; a role play allows students to show empathy for different points of view and demonstrate their acting skills, if they have any (although those particular skills might not be graded).

Student choice

Giving students choices in assignment tasks is worth thinking about. Choices allow students to personalise the task, selecting topics that are of more interest to them, or taking an approach that allows them to demonstrate their individual experiences and expertise in unique and creative ways. Rideout (2017) describes an interesting study in which over 2,000 students were invited to choose from a selection of assignments, as well as to adjust the **weighting** of different parts of the submissions. Whether or not students chose differently from the suggested teacher-designed scheme, there was no significant impact on grades. However, student satisfaction with the option of choice was high. Part 3 includes ideas for offering student choice in different assignment tasks.

Group or individual assessment

You need to decide whether the students will work alone on the task or in a group. You may not be the one to choose this: many, if not most, contemporary university courses have a programme learning outcome which states that students will be able to work in teams by the end of the course. The rationale for this is to support the development of team-working skills, which are generally considered to be important in life after university. Group work can be used to assess any of the following outcomes:

- Research, analyse information, and prepare summaries for peers
- Agree a collective outcome
- Take on different roles in a group
- Create something as a group
- Manage their time effectively, set deadlines, and manage outcomes within deadlines
- Accept and fulfil agreed responsibilities among their peers
- Give and receive feedback from peers

To assess this, programme teams will usually include a group task for at least one module assignment, in which students work in groups to prepare their summative assessment. Assignment topics which work well to assess these kinds of outcomes might be things like the analysis of a complex professional situation, a case study of a multidisciplinary team, problem-solving which requires several leads to be followed up, or organising an event. You can use a wide variety of task types and each task in Part 3 indicates its suitability for group work.

Group assessment can cause a great deal of anxiety for students, especially if it counts significantly to the final degree classification. Anecdotally, I've heard many teachers report that they find managing group assessment to be challenging, and that students frequently complain about its fairness. Gibbs (2009) provides a good overview of ways to avoid problems with the allocation of marks, and when these suggestions are applied, group assessment seems to be extremely effective. At least one study has found no difference in student satisfaction between students who did and didn't experience group work, and that participating in group work had a positive effect on progression (Gamlath, 2021).

If you are using group assessment, a key decision is about what it is you want to assess. Is it the process of working in a team, the product they jointly produce, or a mixture of both? The selection of the best approach is based on various considerations. If this is the main task for a high credit value final-year unit, the groups are of mixed ability, and the students are unfamiliar with group-work processes, then sharing a mark equally between everyone in the group will cause a great deal of anxiety and this could distract students from a focus on the tasks and activities required. Figure 5.1 indicates factors which might be used to decide your approach.

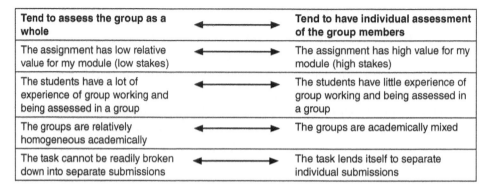

Tend to assess the group as a whole	Tend to have individual assessment of the group members
The assignment has low relative value for my module (low stakes)	The assignment has high value for my module (high stakes)
The students have a lot of experience of group working and being assessed in a group	The students have little experience of group working and being assessed in a group
The groups are relatively homogeneous academically	The groups are academically mixed
The task cannot be readily broken down into separate submissions	The task lends itself to separate individual submissions

Figure 5.1 Factors to consider when planning the assessment of group work

Source: Based on Marr and Forsyth (2010)

If you're marking students individually for their group work, think about what they can produce to show their own work: is it a fraction of a full submission, or are they separate pieces which stand alone? Think carefully about whether grading five minutes of a 25-minute group presentation would really be useful. If you are going to give a group mark to the whole piece, you will be trusting them to contribute equally to the preparation, or you could weight the mark depending on individual perceptions of contribution to the team, or by adding a smaller individual task. If using perceptions of contribution, you need to agree criteria with the students in advance, and Heathfield (1999) suggests criteria such as regular attendance at group meetings, contribution of ideas, researching material for the task, supporting and encouraging each other, and so on. Figure 5.2 provides a summary of possible options for allocating marks. All of the criteria need to be included in the assignment brief, so that students know what to expect and how to discuss any difficulties with you.

And finally, you will need to have an alternative task available for individuals to complete, to accommodate issues such as student illness or other absence or irrevocable breakdown of relationships in a group.

Tend to assess the group as a whole			Tend to have individual assessment of the group members
Sharing the same mark equally between all members of the group	Sharing a proportion of the total available mark equally and allocating the remainder according to the group's perception of individual contributions to the task	Sharing a proportion of the total available mark equally and allocating the remainder for an individual submission which reflects on the process of completing the group task	Asking for individual submissions related to the task and marking these rather than marking a group submission

Figure 5.2 Options for allocating group marks

Submission size

You will need to specify the size of the assignment: the number of words for a written piece, or the number of minutes for a presentation, or the size of a poster or an exhibition space, for instance. It is important to give students a sense of what is expected, to help them to put parameters on what is expected. This could be the most challenging decision you make about assessment, or it could be the easiest. Your university may have set assignment sizes for different types of assignment, which makes the decision simple, unless you disagree with the recommendations, of course. If you have free rein to choose, or you have selected an assignment task which is not yet commonly used, then the decision is a little more complicated.

Custom and practice is a good place to start. Assignments of the same type on the same course should normally be comparable in size, otherwise students may become very confused about expectations. You can look at similar assignments in your own university or elsewhere – many universities publish course outlines which include this level of detail.

Think about how much time the students should spend on preparing their assignment submission: a rule of thumb I have used is to say that working directly on the assignment should take up about 25% of the time available for the module. In the UK system, 1 credit point is nominally associated with 10 hours of student work, so for a 10 credit (5 ECTS credits) module associated with 100 hours of student learning, the student should spend 25 hours on the assignment. This gives you a basis for estimating how much they can realistically do in that time, including all reading, data collection, analysis, and so on. Thinking through the stages which might be needed for the assignment will also help you to break down the processes you think will need to be completed and to explain them to colleagues and to students. This will also give you a clear line of reasoning so that you can peer review your estimates by talking through your design decisions with a colleague, which will help to refine your thinking.

However, whatever approach is taken, it will just be a rule of thumb: all the studies done on student workload shows that there is a huge variation between individual students as to the time it takes to actually complete assignments and as to students' perception of how much time it takes (Crook & Park, 2004; Kember, 2004; Kember & Leung, 2006; Sastry & Bekhradnia, 2007). It is therefore important to give students a clear idea of how long you think it might take them to complete the assigned work, sharing your thoughts about each stage of the process, but also to make it clear that there will be significant individual variations.

Penalties for overlong assignments

Submissions which are longer than expected present a difficulty to staff for three reasons:

1   They take longer to mark.
2   Students who use more words, or time, or space, may be at an advantage over those who have kept to the specified assignment length.
3   There may be a skill being tested by keeping to the specified assignment length.

Some universities or courses may penalise students for producing an assignment which is larger than the size specified in the assignment brief. Applying a penalty to submissions which vary from the recommended size is an effective way to mitigate the effect of these problems. There are two ways to do this. You can ignore any material after the cut-off point, marking only the part of the assignment from the beginning to the specified assignment length, so that you are not marking the full piece. This requires you to measure the length yourself (for instance, cutting off a presentation after the indicated time, or counting the number of words of pages you have in front of you), which may be inconvenient. If you are using this penalty with a written submission, your task is easier if you frame it in terms of the number of pages you will mark, specifying the font and margin sizes so that all students present work in the same way. Do be aware that you may find it difficult to apply marking criteria reliably to a partial piece of work when the rest of the work is actually available to you.

The second approach is to apply a penalty such as reducing the mark by a set amount depending on how much larger it is. There may be rules about this in your own institution, or you can use a tariff like the one in Table 5.4. Again, you will have to measure the length yourself, apply the penalty, and indicate in the feedback what has been done, which can be time-consuming. You need to think about the balance of effort for you as well as for the students compared to the importance you put on a tight word count.

You might choose to use a penalty in order to achieve consistency and fairness, as well as to manage your time more effectively, but be aware that the use of very tightly worded penalties can encourage some undesirable behaviours, such as the removal of important grammatical words to hit the target, affecting the flow or sense of the work.

Table 5.4 Indicative tariff for penalising overlong assignments

Amount the submitted work is in excess of the provided guidance	Effect on final mark
0% – 10%	None
11% – 20%	Mark reduced by 5%
21% – 30%	Mark reduced by 10%
> 31%	Mark capped at pass

You can mitigate this by using a range rather than a strict cut-off for the assignment size: 2,500–3,000 words, or 5–6 minutes, or within an area of 1 × 2 metres, for instance. This gives students the sense of a desirable range rather than a perfect target.

You could also apply a penalty for submissions which are smaller than the recommended size, but this may be less important. A concise but brilliant piece may merit a high grade, while a short and inadequate one would penalise itself by not meeting all of the learning outcomes to a level sufficient to achieve a high mark. If you are applying a penalty, make sure that you explain its purpose and the way you will apply it in the assignment brief.

Students with a disability which affects their language processing may be adversely affected by the application of strict penalties, particularly if writing under time pressures. If you can, discuss penalties with disability advisors to see if adjustments may need to be made.

The final point to make on the topic of the size of the submission is to decide whether references, subheadings, and the words in figures, tables, and diagrams are included in the totals. These can make a significant difference. Usually, you want to mark the main content of the assignment rather than the size of these items, so it does make sense to exclude them from an academic point of view. However, if the number of references or the contents of a diagram are important to the task, this could be specified as part of the assignment brief and you can make it clear that you are increasing the main assessment size accordingly.

Attendance policies

It is common in some countries to include an attendance or participation policy as part of the assignment task. There are two principal ways to do this: either a percentage of the task is allocated to attendance or participation, or the student is not allowed to access the assignment task if they have not attended a minimum number of classes or participated in class activities according to a specified description. The usual intention of such policies is to emphasise the individual or group benefits of class attendance. There is a definite correlation between attendance and achievement, so you could well argue that it is in the student's best interest to attend (Halpern, 2007; Newman-Ford et al., 2008;

Sund & Bignoux, 2018). Attendance is also likely to promote group identity and help to develop good relationships between students and between staff and students. For some professional qualifications, a minimum attendance at certain types of session may be required for the final award.

This kind of policy is clearly problematic in an outcome-based system. Attendance is impossible to include in a learning outcome in higher education – it can be an outcome, but no learning is required to turn up to class. If you include such a requirement, you are reducing the marks available for the actual learning outcomes. You also can't give attendance a grade – either the student meets the requirement, or they don't. So that element of the task can only be given a pass or fail, or 100% or 0%. How does that fit into your grading system?

Even if you can accommodate these difficulties with outcomes and grades, an attendance policy may reinforce difficulties that students already have. Students' reasons for attendance or non-attendance are complex (Menendez Alvarez-Hevia et al., 2018; Oldfield et al., 2017). Suppose your student works to pay for their fees and living expenses, and their manager has a rota where they absolutely have to work on the day of the class one week in four, or risk losing the job? Or if they suffer from regular illness which makes attendance occasionally difficult? Or if they accompany a parent to hospital treatment one day a month, which clashes with the class?

Of course, you can decide on your own boundaries for acceptable excuses and make exceptions, but why not have an inclusive policy so that students are in a position to succeed in your class without having to ask for special treatment? Attendance and participation are clearly important features of curriculum design, but in relation to the topic of the book, you need to decide whether they feature in your assessment policy or whether you encourage them through other means.

Timing

You need to make a decision about any assignment which is timed to be completed or submitted during the module. This applies to both summative and formative assessment carried out during the module. Perhaps you only have one assignment per module, in which case the submission date will usually be towards or at the end of the teaching period. The last assignment in a module will also usually be at or after the end of the module. It might be that your university has set periods when assessments can be completed, which makes the decision easy for you.

If the first assignment is a preparation for the final assignment, you will need to think particularly carefully about when in the module would be most useful to the student, as well as most manageable for you. If you want to give rapid feedback to students so that they can improve their final work, you need to have a submission date that gives you time to produce meaningful feedback, taking into account your other commitments.

Avoiding academic misconduct

It is impossible to design out the possibility of academic misconduct completely, and we will look at detection of dishonesty in Chapter 7, but there are some steps you can take in the design of an assignment to reduce the likelihood of plagiarism or the use of contract cheating. Bretag et al. (2019) surveyed students on the likelihood that they would use a contract cheating service for different types of assignment tasks, and found that those tasks least likely to prompt contract cheating were in-class tasks, personalised and unique tasks, vivas, and reflections on practical placements. A 2001 guide (Carroll & Appleton, 2001) still covers all of the important factors in trying to design out opportunities for plagiarism, and although contract cheating was relatively undocumented at the time it was written, there is correlation between their advice and these findings. The key suggestions made by Carroll and Appleton are:

1 Change assignments regularly

If you set similar essay titles, problems, or laboratory reports each year, you are making it a lot easier for the student with good social contacts to find and reproduce a submission from a previous year.

2 Create individualised tasks

The use of open and creative learning outcomes should make it easier to set assignment tasks that can be personalised. Carroll and Appleton (2001, p. 10) say that 'Assessing application or comparison rather than use will encourage more individualised products'. You can ask students to perform a transformational task (e.g. rewriting, synthesising, or summarising several texts) and then to write a short, reflective piece summarising their approach and reasoning. Other possibilities might include requiring students to select their best contributions to an online discussion and asking them to accompany the selection with a commentary, or asking them to make links from a topic to current events or publications so that the work needs to have contemporary context.

For modules which necessarily have closed learning outcomes relating to knowledge acquisition, varying the questions between years and between individuals can reduce the possibility of cheating. For instance, if you are setting mathematical problems, you can use online assessment software which generates a bank of questions with randomly selected values for different variables, allowing you to vary the questions between individuals without increased effort on your part. A less conventional approach would be to set the task of asking students to set problems for each other rather than simply solving them. You could also set problems related to topics in the news, so that they are unlikely to find exact equivalents elsewhere.

3 Incorporate drafts into the assessment process

There are two benefits to this strategy: first, you will be helping the students with poor time management skills to plan and structure their work, and second, you will get an idea of the students' capabilities as they progress through the task, which should make glaring differences in the final product obvious. Looking at drafts is work for you which needs to be incorporated into your teaching planning, and which may be impossible with large cohorts. We will look at the process in more detail in Chapter 6. You can ease the burden by seeing drafts in the forms of short bulleted lists, poster displays, or presentations.

4 Vary the tasks and assess process rather than product

Traditional university assignments tend to be based on products such as an essay, art-work, or presentation. If you incorporate process into the grading of the task as well, you can reduce opportunities for plagiarism as well as indicating the importance of working towards a final product in developing essential graduate skills. This is a basic element of art and design education, when the sketchbook or portfolio is frequently assessed along-side the piece of artwork which is submitted for assessment. In other contexts, you can ask for an essay plan together with an annotated bibliography for a full essay, or a description of the process of preparing an assignment, or a reflection on what has been learned. In science, you can ask for a set of outline lab reports alongside one completed one.

5 Education

When students and academic staff were asked to rate 'wrong-doing' in various forms, including academic dishonesty, students consistently took wrong-doing less seriously than academic staff (Dardoy, 2002). This suggests that informing students is not enough: they need to subscribe to our view of academic honesty as well. This can be explained in handbooks and supplemented by subject-based discussion of plagiarism. Why is it a prob-lem in your subject? What are the consequences for individuals? For the institution? For the intended profession? What are the differences between collaboration and collusion? What does the department do to detect plagiarism?

As suggested by Bretag et al. (2019), you can also use supervised, time-constrained, examinations such as in-class tests and oral examinations to ensure that the person being assessed is presenting the work. These are not, however, a perfect solution. They don't guarantee that the student completed the work themselves, as they may have memo-rised someone else's work, and time-constrained assessment is not always suitable for the learning outcomes you seek to assess, and it can be very stressful for students with certain disabilities or illnesses.

As part of your assignment planning, you should think about what will happen if you do suspect academic dishonesty during the marking process. Your university will have regulations about the detection process, and the penalties for dishonesty, so do check these first if you aren't familiar with them. You could build in the option of a short additional interview or oral examination to confirm the students' personal mastery of the learning outcomes, if this is possible within your university's regulations and if there is time within the marking period. The possibility of using such an additional test would need to be signalled as part of the assignment brief, which is why it is mentioned in this chapter, but we will return to their use in Chapter 7.

If possible, it is useful to involve a range of other people in thinking about your new assignment task. Colleagues are an obvious choice, and may have tried whatever it is you are thinking about before, but you can also discuss with potential employers, representatives from professional bodies, ex-students, and current students. They are likely to have views about the value and manageability of your proposals which will help you to refine the ideas. It's also worth considering that if you are not very confident about introducing a new type of task, then you could consider using it formatively to begin with, and then make it a summative assessment in a future year.

Anonymous submissions

Anonymous marking is carried out when the marker does not know the identity of the student whose work they are grading. As with group work, you may not have choices over whether you employ this or not, as your university may have a policy which requires it. The rationale for anonymous marking is that it removes bias: you are simply marking what is in front of you, which is of course what is expected in an outcomes-based system of marking. The argument against it is that it depersonalises feedback and discourages the provision of feedback on drafts, because the tutor would then recognise the submission (Winstone & Boud, 2020). Recent research has tended to show that using anonymous marking or not does not have a significant effect on student progression or overall grades compared to non-anonymised marking (Hinton & Higson, 2017; Pitt & Winstone, 2018), but it really is an under-researched area.

Some kinds of submission, such as those that are event-based (presentations, performances, poster sessions, and so on), are clearly unsuitable for anonymous marking, but it should be possible for most digital submissions. If using the approach, you will need to think about how you plan marking and feedback, and the submission process must include a way to remove the identifying details but still retain the ability to reunite the student with their corrected work and their grade. Most digital submission systems should have this built in. With paper submissions such as examination papers, students often have to cover over their name with an adhesive patch which can be removed after marking.

Conclusion

Effective assessment design is complex and context-dependent. The choice of the type and size of assignment task needs to take into account subject and university custom and practice, professional requirements, your own workload and motivations, the support you have from colleagues, and the needs and attributes of the students in your university. And of course, each assignment task must allow students to demonstrate their achievement of learning outcomes at the right level. There is no perfect solution – do your best, and plan to review the design with colleagues and students after the first time you try it out.

Further reading

For practical guidance on group work, see Moon (2009). There are some good examples of effective group work in Maiden and Perry (2011), who address the problem of 'free-riding' in groups, Hannaford's (2016) report on a case study where the design of the group work seemed effective in making the assessment particularly successful, and Fearon et al. (2012), who designed group work to replicate a professional community of practice.

For a masterful, if unsettling, guide to all aspects of assessment security, spend some time with Dawson's (2020) comprehensive overview.

References

Bretag, T., Harper, R., Burton, M., Ellis, C., Newton, P., van Haeringen, K., Saddiqui, S., & Rozenberg, P. (2019). Contract cheating and assessment design: Exploring the relationship. *Assessment & Evaluation in Higher Education*, 44(5), 676–691. https://doi.org /10.1080/02602938.2018.1527892

Carroll, J., & Appleton, J. (2001). *Plagiarism: A good practice guide*. Oxford: Oxford Brookes University.

Crook, A. C., & Park, J. R. (2004). Measuring assessment: A methodology for investigating undergraduate assessment. *Bioscience Education e-Journal*, 4(6). www.bioscience. heacademy.ac.uk/journal/vol4/beej-4-6.pdf

Dardoy, A. (2002). *Cheating and plagiarism: Student and staff perceptions at Northumbria*. Northumbria Conference – Educating for the Future, November.

Dawson, P. (2020). *Defending assessment security in a digital world: Preventing e-cheating and supporting academic integrity in higher education*. Abingdon: Routledge.

Fearon, C., McLaughlin, H., & Eng, T. Y. (2012). Using student group work in higher education to emulate professional communities of practice. *Education + Training*, 54(2/3), 114–125. https://doi.org/doi:10.1108/00400911211210233

Gamlath, S. (2021). Business undergraduates' progress and satisfaction with learning experiences: The role of group assessment. *Assessment & Evaluation in Higher Education*, 46(3), 360–375. https://doi.org/10.1080/02602938.2020.1776839

Gibbs, G. (2009). The assessment of group work: Lessons from the literature. *Assessment Standards Knowledge Exchange*, 1–17.

Halpern, N. (2007). The impact of attendance and student characteristics on academic achievement: Findings from an undergraduate business management module. *Journal of Further and Higher Education*, 31(4), 335–349. www.informaworld. com/10.1080/03098770701626017

Hannaford, L. (2016). Motivation in group assessment: A phenomenological approach to post-graduate group assessment. *Assessment & Evaluation in Higher Education*, 1–14. https://doi.org/10.1080/02602938.2016.1195787

Heathfield, M. (1999). Group-based assessment: An evaluation of the use of assessed tasks as a method of fostering high quality learning. In S. Brown & A. Glasner (Eds.), *Assessment matters in higher education* (pp. 132–145). Buckingham: Open University Press/SRHE.

Hinton, D. P., & Higson, H. (2017). A large-scale examination of the effectiveness of anonymous marking in reducing group performance differences in higher education assessment. *PLoS ONE*, *12*(8), e0182711. https://doi.org/10.1371/journal.pone.0182711

Kember, D. (2004). Interpreting student workload and the factors which shape students' perceptions of their workload. *Studies in Higher Education*, *29*(2), 165–184. www.informaworld.com/10.1080/0307507042000190778

Kember, D., & Leung, D. Y. P. (2006). Characterising a teaching and learning environment conducive to making demands on students while not making their workload excessive. *Studies in Higher Education*, *31*(2), 185–198. www.informaworld.com/10.1080/03075070600572074

Maiden, B., & Perry, B. (2011). Dealing with free-riders in assessed group work: Results from a study at a UK university. *Assessment & Evaluation in Higher Education*, *36*(4), 451–464. https://doi.org/10.1080/02602930903429302

Marr, L., & Forsyth, R. (2010). *Identity crisis: Working in HE in the 21st century*. Stoke-on-Trent: Trentham Books.

Menendez Alvarez-Hevia, D., Lord, J., & Naylor, S. (2018). Being there? A collaborative inquiry into attendance. *Fourth International Conference on Higher Education Advances (HEAd'18), Valencia*, June, https://doi.org/10.4995/HEAd18.2018.7899.

Moon, J. (2009). *Making groups work*. http://escalate.ac.uk/downloads/5413.pdf

Newman-Ford, L., Fitzgibbon, K., Lloyd, S., & Thomas, S. (2008). A large-scale investigation into the relationship between attendance and attainment: A study using an innovative, electronic attendance monitoring system. *Studies in Higher Education*, *33*(6), 699–717. www.informaworld.com/10.1080/03075070802457066

Nieminen, J. H. (2022). Assessment for inclusion: Rethinking inclusive assessment in higher education. *Teaching in Higher Education*, 1–19. https://doi.org/10.1080/13562517.2021.2021395

Oldfield, J., Rodwell, J., Curry, L., & Marks, G. (2017). A face in a sea of faces: Exploring university students' reasons for non-attendance to teaching sessions. *Journal of Further and Higher Education*, 1–10. https://doi.org/10.1080/0309877X.2017.1363387

Pitt, E., & Winstone, N. (2018). The impact of anonymous marking on students' perceptions of fairness, feedback and relationships with lecturers. *Assessment & Evaluation in Higher Education*, 1–11. https://doi.org/10.1080/02602938.2018.1437594

Rideout, C. A. (2017). Students' choices and achievement in large undergraduate classes using a novel flexible assessment approach. *Assessment & Evaluation in Higher Education*, 1–11. https://doi.org/10.1080/02602938.2017.1294144

Sastry, T., & Bekhradnia, B. (2007). *The Academic Experience of Students in English Universities*. HEPI number 3, 25 September. Oxford: Higher Education Policy Institute. www.hepi.ac.uk/pubdetail.asp?ID=240&DOC=Reports

Scull, P. (2001). An evaluation of the module guides and assignment briefs used in the School of Art and Design (SAD). CELT Learning and Teaching Projects 2000/2001. *University of Wolverhampton*. https://wlv.openrepository.com/handle/2436/6121

Sund, K. J., & Bignoux, S. (2018). Can the performance effect be ignored in the attendance policy discussion? *Higher Education Quarterly*, *72*(4), 360–374. https://doi.org/https://doi.org/10.1111/hequ.12172

Villarroel, V., Bloxham, S., Bruna, D., Bruna, C., & Herrera-Seda, C. (2018). Authentic assessment: Creating a blueprint for course design. *Assessment & Evaluation in Higher Education*, *43*(5), 840–854. https://doi.org/10.1080/02602938.2017.1412396

Winstone, N. E., & Boud, D. (2020). The need to disentangle assessment and feedback in higher education. *Studies in Higher Education*, 1–12. https://doi.org/10.1080/03075079.2020.1779687

6
DESIGNING EFFECTIVE MARKING AND FEEDBACK

Chapter overview

This chapter explores:

- Developing marking criteria or schemes
- Planning a feedback strategy
- Planning a moderation strategy

Introduction

Planning your marking and feedback strategy is a key part of preparing yourself and your students for both teaching and assessment. If you have a clear idea of how you are going to judge student submissions and what you expect students to do with the feedback they receive, you can build that information into the work you do together to prepare the assignments. Moderation of assessed work is a key part of **mitigations** to reduce uncertainty in the assessment process, and can be built into the overall planning. This chapter looks in detail at the decisions you need to take in making these plans.

Marking criteria

An assignment description is incomplete without an indication of how it will be marked (graded) to show the degree to which a student has achieved the learning outcomes tested in the assignment task. The production and use of criteria is therefore important but, in practice, Bloxham et al. (2011) found that many teachers did not make direct use of criteria while they were marking student work, although some did refer back to criteria to support a judgement about grades. This doesn't mean that the criteria are meaningless but, more likely, that teachers are working with socially constructed standards, which become part of their tacit knowledge. If this is the case, then criteria are the way in which these standards are shared with people new to the community – students and novice teachers – and they should be very carefully written to ensure that they are understood.

Institutional practices may vary, but, if possible, you should write criteria which are specific to the assignment task. Each task tests different learning outcomes, and so it is logical to use marking criteria that are adapted to these outcomes and to the level of study. It is worth spending time on your marking criteria and on reviewing them regularly; clear, usable criteria will make the task of making judgements easier and will facilitate conversations about what you are expecting with both students and colleagues who are working with you to mark and moderate submissions.

The simplest set of marking criteria has two grades: pass (student has met the learning outcomes) and fail (student has not met the learning outcomes). As we noted in Chapter 3, there are different systems for higher education grading around the world, but they are mostly more complex schemes than pass/fail; using a range of grades is intended to discriminate between students, and to allow teachers to reward students who have done much more than simply pass. There are two basic approaches to this: a holistic scheme, which judges the whole piece of work submitted by the student, or an analytical scheme, which allocates parts of the total grade to different parts of the assignment. The choice should be made according to the level of the work and the type of assignment.

Rubrics

There are various grading tools which are identified as rubrics (Dawson, 2017) but we will use a simple description, which is that a marking rubric is a grid which provides criteria for judging an assignment and a scale for judging different levels of student performance. Rubrics can be used to convert judgements to grades (quantitative use) or simply to indicate characteristics of the submission (qualitative use), but in most situations you will be using a rubric to provide a grade, so we will assume that this is the case. If you are only providing feedback, then the process of writing the rubric will be exactly the same as the one described here, but you won't put grades against the column headings.

In the rest of the section, we'll illustrate rubrics using a grid which has what is to be assessed listed in rows, with the differential performance measures in columns, but of course you can equally write them the other way round; you will decide based on convention (it's easier for students if all of their teachers use the same style), preference, and appearance. Rubrics are a helpful way to share expectations with students and colleagues, but care needs to be taken to construct them so that they lead to shared understandings (Chan & Ho, 2019; Kite & Phongsavan, 2016).

Rubrics can be used in two principal ways: they can divide the assignment into component parts, with a section for each part (an analytical scheme), or they can have a row for each of the learning outcomes for the assignment (a holistic scheme). There is a third approach, which is based on generic outcomes, but this is less common. It is a holistic approach, and would be designed in a similar way to the learning outcome approach, but substituting the module learning outcomes for these generic ones, so we won't cover it separately. It is described in Cullen et al. (2016) if you want to see examples.

Matshedisho (2019, p. 9) found gaps between teacher intention and student interpretation of rubrics, which they characterised as a gap between 'students' desire for procedural knowledge and the lecturer's expectation of conceptual knowledge', which is a helpful way of considering misunderstandings. In this study, students explained their confusions about the use of academic language that they found ambiguous, and what it meant to write reflectively. A teacher using reflective writing in assignments is unlikely to have views on what a 'correct' answer looks like, but students wanted to be given examples of correct answers. This point about teacher and student expectations is considered further in Chapter 7 when we look at the use of exemplars, but for now the focus is on producing unambiguous criteria in both analytical and holistic rubrics.

Analytical schemes

An analytical scheme is used when a range of accurate knowledge or competent skills needs to be tested. Effectively, analytical schemes make a series of pass/fail decisions across a range of smaller tasks, with the final grade depending on the number of successes. The discrimination between students is therefore achieved on the breadth of knowledge or skills. You might choose an analytical scheme if your learning outcomes use words such as define, identify, calculate, or select (unistructural outcomes according to the SOLO taxonomy (Biggs & Collis, 1982), or remember/understand in Bloom's Taxonomy (1956).

The approach would be suitable for a set of short numerical problems, for instance, or a practical or clinical examination with certain defined steps which must be followed; an example of a rubric for a clinical examination is shown in Table 6.1. A multiple-choice test would represent the use of an analytical scheme, with a defined number of marks available for each correct answer. For safety critical assessments, a mark of 100% might be required on an analytical scheme in order to achieve a pass.

These schemes are usually more suitable at lower levels of study where a foundation of knowledge and expertise is being built. There are exceptions to this, when students at higher levels are developing new knowledge: assessment in UK medical schools is almost entirely based on analytical schemes using multiple-choice questions or clinical examinations which become progressively more complex as the student proceeds. Table 6.1 shows a relatively simple rubric which requires the student to have mastered complex underpinning and knowledge to demonstrate the competences which are assessed.

Table 6.1 Example of an analytical scheme (clinical situation)

Grade Competence	Could not be improved	Pass	Fail
Introduces self to patient	Includes all relevant details and explains what they will be doing during the consultation. Patient clearly set at ease.	Basic but clear introduction to self and role. Patient has limited opportunity to speak.	Misses important information about self or role. Patient has no opportunity to ask for clarification.
Takes appropriate history	Asks about everything relevant and explains why they are asking. Asks if they have missed anything and allows patient to contribute things they think are important.	Asks about everything relevant. Patient has limited opportunity to speak or add information.	Does not ask about everything important to the case. Patient has no opportunity to speak or add information.
Checks pattern of recent test results	Talks patient through the meaning of recent results and why they are important.	Considers test results accurately but is mainly aiming at the examiner.	Misses important information from the test results. Does not share meaning with patient.
Suggests appropriate treatment plan	An appropriate treatment plan is proposed and explained to the patient, with appropriate links to relevant research.	An appropriate treatment plan is proposed. It is not expressed in everyday terms.	An inadequate treatment plan is proposed.
Allows patient to ask questions	Able to manage and respond well to patient questions, reassuring them and explaining how they will get answers if they are unable to respond immediately.	Limited opportunity for patient to ask questions, and/ or limited ability to respond.	No opportunity for patient to ask questions, and/or inadequate responses.

Table 6.2 Example of an analytical scheme (report situation)

Grade Element	Highest grade	Pass	Fail
Abstract	Succinct and interesting summary of the submission.	Summary covers main points of submission clearly.	Summary misses out main points of submission or is unclear or includes content not actually covered.
Introduction	Uses a range of contemporary and relevant sources to contextualise the work.	Uses a satisfactory number of sources to contextualise the work in a basic way.	Inadequate number of sources and/or has not linked the sources to the work effectively.
Method	Clear, succinct summary of what was done. Diagrams used to improve explanation.	Adequate summary of what was done. Diagrams are satisfactory but may not add to the readers' understanding.	Misses out important steps or mis-describes them. Diagrams wrong or non-existent.
Results	Results are clearly and cogently presented, with appropriate use of diagrams or graphical summaries.	Results are adequately presented, with some use of diagrams or graphical summaries.	Results are missing or wrong, with no or incorrect use of diagrams or graphical summaries.
Conclusion	The conclusions link context and results convincingly. Creative and developmental suggestions for future work are made. Limitations are well understood and discussed in detail.	The conclusions link context and results plausibly. Some suggestions for future work are made. Limitations are correctly identified and discussed.	The conclusions do not link context and results clearly. No or inadequate suggestions for future work are made. Limitations are poorly understood or absent from discussion.
References	Correct use of required citation format.	Correct use of required citation format.	Incorrect use of required citation format.

These examples are not intended to be perfect exemplars; they are fairly simplistic and are included only to demonstrate process. You will definitely be able to improve on them. Table 6.2 also demonstrates the difficulty of making judgements on simple situations, such as correct use of referencing: how can you allocate a full range of grades to something which is basically correct or incorrect? However, I have included it, as I often see it in analytical schemes, and you may want to think about whether it should be there or not when assessing at undergraduate level, or whether you will include consideration of it in a learning outcome about communication of ideas.

Another type of analytical scheme involves the selection of components that should be in the assignment. The components could be structural elements, such as introduction, literature review, argument, discussion, conclusions, references, or they could be essential parts, such as knowledge and understanding, analysis, use of resources, structure, and use of language (see Bloxham & Boyd, 2007, p. 91; or Rublee, 2014, p. 3, for examples of these).

Holistic schemes

A holistic marking scheme provides the basis for making judgements about the characteristics of the complete submission. You would choose this when you have expected students to process information into a new perspective or judgement of their own, with learning outcome verbs such as explain, analyse, synthesise, create, design, and so on (these would be considered as multi-structural and upwards with the SOLO taxonomy (Biggs & Collis, 1982), or apply, analyse, evaluate, and create with Anderson and Krathwohl's revision of Bloom's Taxonomy (Anderson & Krathwohl, 2001)).

The first step in writing a criterion for a holistic scheme is to start with one of the learning outcomes, identify what you would like to see in the assignment which has the characteristics of a pass, and then formulate that into a sentence. You also need to take account of the level of study when thinking about the breadth and depth of your expectations. This will be partially accounted for in the learning outcomes, but think about how many data sources you would expect, or the type of audience the student is preparing work for, or the level of reflection that would be appropriate at the level of study. Table 6.3 gives generic examples of how you might develop expectations for a pass grade in a range of common assessment expectations as students move through higher education in a system with a three-year undergraduate degree.

Table 6.3 Illustration of the progression of expectations through higher education levels

First year	Second year	Third year	Master's
Links between theory and practice are identified.	Links between theory and practice are constructed.	Problems are solved with some reference to theory and practice and with evidence of some critical reflection.	Novel and complex problems are solved with reference to theory and practice.
Ideas are recognisably structured and presented to an audience of peers using a defined range of strategies and media.	Ideas are clearly communicated using a range of strategies and media.	Ideas are presented to a selected audience using a range of strategies and media.	Ideas are presented appropriately to a professional audience using a range of strategies and media.
Information from primary and secondary sources is collected and applied to specific problems under supervision.	A simple project is designed and carried out to collect, analyse, and critique information from primary and secondary sources under supervision.	A complex project is designed, planned, and carried out using an appropriate range of primary and secondary sources. The results and/or outcomes are evaluated accurately.	A professional project is planned and carried out to gather information from appropriate primary and secondary sources and synthesise the results.

If your grading system is pass/fail, you can skip the next step. If you have to produce criteria for a range of grade bands, try to imagine the characteristics of a perfect piece of work at that level and write a sentence to capture this. Table 6.4 shows some first drafts of criteria at different levels of study for some of the sample learning outcomes we used in Chapter 1, so that you can see the rubric beginning to be created.

Table 6.4 First draft of some criteria for the pass and top bands

Learning outcome	Basic pass	Highest grade
Critically analyse existing practice in marking and feedback for a selected unit or programme of study in higher education (master's level).	Gathers information from appropriate sources and synthesises the results to produce a basic analysis of the assignment and make acceptable recommendations.	A complex and innovative analysis of the assessment is produced, which synthesises useful information from a wide range of appropriate sources to produce an original proposal.
Critically analyse results of experiments undertaken to investigate [a specific topic in the subject area] (final-year undergraduate).	Identifies key aspects of the experiments and links them to literature in a coherent way to form a plausible conclusion.	Considers the key aspects of the experiments in relation to a wide range of literature, identifying limitations and making original proposals for future work.
Explain the differences between [different schools of thought in the subject area] (first-year undergraduate).	Provides a basic description of the schools of thought and identifies points of comparison with reference to a small range of sources.	Provides a critical comparison of the schools of thought with reference to a wide range of sources.

Finally, you would fill in the criteria for the grade bands in between pass and perfect, and the criteria which would lead to a fail grade; this last column is often created by explaining what is not present in the failed piece of work. There are good arguments for trying to use positive language in giving feedback, but criteria need to show students clearly how the submission relates to the expectations. If they receive a failing grade, they must be able to see from the rubric what was missing from the work.

As we discussed in Chapter 2, it is almost impossible to remove subjectivity in judgement when marking holistically. However, you can make a conversation about the meaning of criteria easier by keeping a consistent structure for each criterion as you move between the different grade bands, and using meaningful adjectives to differentiate performance between grade bands. This kind of structure will enable you to have more direct conversations about what you are looking for in the work with both students and colleagues who are marking or moderating submissions. Try to avoid words such as excellent, very good, and good if you can, as other people may have very different ideas about what they mean in relation to a task, leading to confusion and less certainty about aiming for a grade (for students) or selecting a grade (for markers). Using more specific adjectives will give a clearer focus. Table 6.5 has some examples for a simple system using five grade bands, but you can use your imagination, and you might well disagree with these categorisations and want to move adjectives between rows. The main aim is for you to be able to explain what distinguishes work placed in different bands.

Table 6.5 Examples of adjectives used to discriminate between grade bands

Grade band	Adjectives
A	Authoritative, convincing, creative*, exciting, illuminating, insightful, inspiring, meticulous, original, persuasive, sophisticated, unexpected
B	Ambitious, critical, fluent, analytical, precise, reflective, rigorous
C	Accurate, coherent, confident, congruent, consistent, thorough, thoughtful
D	Adequate, careful, clear, descriptive**, satisfactory, sufficient
E	Contradictory, derivative, erroneous/wrong, inadequate, inappropriate, incoherent, incomplete, inconsistent, insufficient, irrelevant, limited, superficial

In a creative discipline, 'creative' might be a pass grade (D on this system)
** *Descriptive might be a fail grade at higher levels of study*

Your final task is to decide how to calculate a grade. If you are using a rubric for grading, each box must represent a mark which will contribute to the final grade. You need to decide whether each box in the rubric will have a single grade associated with it, or will you provide a grade for the top, middle, and bottom of the band (Table 6.6)? Are you able to differentiate performance to that level of detail? You are unlikely to be able to be more specific in your judgement than high, mid, or low achievement of the criterion, so don't be tempted to get more detailed than this.

Table 6.6 Possible ways to allocate grades to rubric elements

Learning outcome	Basic pass UK undergraduate system, grade between 40% and 49% Letter system, C	Highest grade UK undergraduate system, grade between 70% and 100% Letter system, A
Critically analyse results of experiments undertaken to investigate [a specific topic in the subject area] (final-year undergraduate)	Identifies key aspects of the experiments and links them to literature in a coherent way to form a plausible conclusion.	Considers the key aspects of the experiments in relation to a wide range of literature, identifying limitations and making original proposals for future work.
Option 1: Everyone with a tick in this box gets the same mark for this criterion: UK system Letter system	45 C	85 A
Option 2: The tick in the box may represent a high, mid, or low achievement for this criterion, so there are possible marks of: UK system Letter system	42, 45, 48 C-, C, C+	75, 85, 95 A-, A, A+

These examples show some of the complexity of working with different grading systems. For option 1, this example uses the grade in the middle of the band on the UK system – 45% for the pass band, and 85% for the highest, first class, band. Hence maximum marks would never be possible using such a rubric. But if you did offer maximum marks for each band, overall grades would probably be skewed upwards from what you intended and from custom and practice. This is an artefact of the UK grade band system, which mixes holistic judgements with mathematical calculation of results from differently sized bands. You may not be reading this book in the UK, and so don't need to think about this. If you are in the UK, as it will take a revolution to move to a more logical system, which would have evenly sized bands and simple calculations of final grades, only guidance on working with it will be provided: use a maximum of three grade points per band, and space these evenly per band, whatever the number of percentage points available to you in the band.

Finally, you need to decide how each row in your rubric contributes to the final grade. If using a holistic rubric, with one row per learning outcome, then you would normally weight them evenly – so if there are four learning outcomes, each row contributes 25% to the final mark for the submission. You may decide to use another formula, if you think that the learning outcomes have differing value in the module, but an equal weighting is probably most straightforward for everyone to understand. With an analytical rubric, you may want to show variation in importance of different elements by weighting the rows differently – for instance, you might think that analysis contributes 30% and referencing is 10% of the value of the assignment.

For all of the reasons we discussed in Chapter 2 about making judgements, writing marking criteria is not a precise science. Bloxham and Boyd (2007) caution strongly against providing too much detail in your rubrics; over-specification gives the illusion of precision in making complex judgements, and may encourage students to look for ways of collecting marks from inclusion of specific details.

You should be prepared to have discussions about the meanings of the criteria with students and colleagues, testing out your own tacit expectations and providing examples of what might be included in a successful submission. You can improve the reliability of your criteria by having them peer-reviewed by colleagues, and trying them out with previous submissions, if available. Once they have been published to students, you will need to stick with them until after marking is complete, but you will almost certainly want to make small changes following the first time you use them with a batch of submissions.

Feedback strategy

Planning a feedback strategy will help you to make sure that you make best use of your time in the marking process, and also help you share with colleagues and students the function of your feedback.

What is good feedback?

When teachers and students are asked about the purpose of feedback on assessed work, there is general agreement that it should be to support improvement (Dawson et al., 2018; O'Donovan et al., 2021; Price et al., 2010), and so good feedback is presumably feedback which is entirely focused on this aim.

Having said that, there is not necessarily agreement on what good feedback looks like. O'Donovan et al. (2021) found that students were influenced in their thinking by their previous experiences, and identified the potential clash between what students expected and the evidence on effective feedback, a point also highlighted by Winstone et al. (2017). Dawson et al. (2018) carried out a large-scale survey of students and staff to identify elements of effective feedback, and found a wide variety in views on what good feedback looks like. Even though traditional approaches to feedback may not be effective, and are certainly criticised by students (Williams et al., 2008), it can be difficult to implement new approaches when there is such a range of expectations. There is a danger that feedback may be used for other purposes, such as to defend the allocation of grades, or to improve student satisfaction, or to conform to an externally designed quality process (Winstone & Carless, 2021), and you may find it difficult to ignore pressures to bend your strategy to these aims. However, we will assume that you have autonomy over your own feedback planning as a starting point; if you have to adapt it to fit with programme, departmental, institutional, or professional body requirements, at least you will have started from a strong foundation.

Boud and Molloy (2012) have argued that positioning feedback for learning offers some clear principles that you can use to develop your own strategy. In brief, consider your feedback as part of a process to shift the agency of feedback from you, as the teacher and provider of feedback, to the student, who is using your comments as part of their overall learning, alongside other resources, including self- and peer assessment. Your feedback strategy needs to balance the aim of improvement, the ability of the student to make use of the feedback, and your own workload and time available to produce and manage the feedback.

Purposes of feedback

We will look at producing feedback on assignments in Chapter 8, but it is important to include your feedback strategy in assignment design. If you have a clear plan for what you will provide to the students and what you expect them to do with that feedback, you will find it easier to produce the feedback and for it to be valuable to students even after they have completed your module. You need to relate this back to your overall aims for the assignment task. In Chapter 1, we pointed out that if judging achievement is the sole purpose, then there is no need for the teacher to provide developmental feedback, suggesting how students might improve in the future.

According to Nicol and Macfarlane-Dick, (2006, p. 203), good feedback practice:

1   helps clarify what good performance is (goals, criteria, expected standards);
2   facilitates the development of self-assessment (reflection) in learning;
3   delivers high quality information to students about their learning;
4   encourages teacher and peer dialogue around learning;
5   encourages positive motivational beliefs and self-esteem;
6   provides opportunities to close the gap between current and desired performance;
7   provides information to teachers that can be used to help shape teaching.

When discussing purpose, it may be useful to think about each of these elements and consider how current practice relates to each of them. Is feedback always produced for the students, or are other audiences sometimes in your mind, such as colleagues who may be second marking, or external examiners? Is the need to motivate students to continue always considered? Can advice on future development be found in every piece of feedback?

Student engagement with feedback

Feedback will only achieve its intended purpose if students use it. Zimbardi et al. (2016) found a link between the length of time students spent engaging with feedback with their subsequent academic performance, suggesting a correlation between effective feedback and development. Chris Rust has observed that:

> ...the emotional and psychological investment in producing a piece of work for assessment has a much stronger effect on the student than the relatively passive receipt of subsequent feedback. Consequently, if asked to repeat the task sometime later, the student is likely to replicate what they did the first time, including the mistakes, despite the fact that these were pointed out, and supposedly 'corrected' in the feedback. (Rust, 2002, p. 153)

Since then, there has been plenty of research into what works in designing feedback which engages students.

There is some evidence that dialogic approaches to feedback, where the student responds to tutor feedback, can help students to situate feedback within their own study practices and planning (Blair et al., 2014; Carless & Chan, 2016; Hill & West, 2020; Nicol, 2010). These interventions are usually employed in formative assessment, and can be difficult to implement with summative assessment in mass higher education, where feedback is often given after a module has ended and it may be difficult to organise or resource further engagement with the students.

Ahmed Shafi et al. (2017, p. 423) found that students used feedback in a variety of constructive ways, including 'to manage their emotions when a disappointing grade was received'. This leads to the question of what ingredients are needed for students to make good use of the feedback. Winstone et al. (2017, p. 2031) suggest that four psychological processes are needed for students to engage effectively with feedback: awareness, cognisance, agency, and volition. In their study, they found that students understood the purpose of feedback (awareness and cognisance), but didn't always take responsibility for acting on it (agency and volition). There has been some work done with small groups of students that suggests that the emotional impact of feedback may have an effect on students' ability to act, demotivating students if the tone is negative (e.g. Pitt & Norton, 2016; Shields, 2015). Forsythe and Johnson (2016) linked students' ability to use feedback effectively to their existing mindset, with those open to their own improvement and development more able to respond constructively, and those with a fixed view of their own capability more likely to be defensive and dismissive of feedback.

These findings may be related to the ability to self-regulate. This supposition is reinforced by a literature review carried out by Ajjawi et al. (2021, p. 9), which found that 'feedback interventions that met student needs for relatedness, autonomy and/or competence motivated students to engage with feedback processes and therefore mobilised outcomes including improved performance, developing evaluative judgement, self-efficacy and learning'.

A slightly simpler model can be found in Boud and Molloy (2012), who suggest three stages in feedback development, which they call Marks, in reference to iterations of engineering designs. Mark 0 feedback is an adjunct to grading. It is feedback done by teachers to students; teachers hope it is used, and no direct response from students is required or expected. Its main purpose is to justify the mark given.

Mark 1 feedback is the next level. This is more focused on student improvement, and teachers write it to change student behaviour. There might be lots of it, and an open invitation to come and discuss it. Boud and Molloy point out that this model is potentially unsustainable, in terms of teacher time, if students all take up the offer. While the aim is to support improvement for the next assignment, students remain dependent on the teacher to keep providing feedback, and don't develop skills to make use of the feedback by themselves. In Boud and Molloy's view, Mark 2 feedback is needed. Such feedback will contain illustrations, answers, and explanations, but it won't tell students what to do next; it encourages them to form their own ideas. Of course, this recommendation also reflects the notion of the self-regulated learner.

Quantity of feedback

It would be easy to assume that improving feedback simply means providing more feedback, but this isn't necessarily the case. There are many factors involved in the provision of effective feedback (i.e. feedback that students actually go on and use to help them to improve). One thousand words of feedback on an essay, however carefully crafted, will be fairly useless if it's received after the deadline for the next assignment submission. Equally, some students find it very difficult to engage with certain types of feedback for a variety of reasons, and for those students, producing more feedback will not improve their engagement with it. As Knight and Yorke (2003, p. 129) have pointed out, 'lack of success is likely to discourage performance-oriented students, whereas those who are learning-oriented are stimulated to further success'.

Those of us old enough to remember assignments submitted on paper will all be familiar with the sight of uncollected assignments, probably marked under pressure of a deadline, and filled with helpful comments which may never be read. Zimbardi et al. (2016) looked at student engagement with feedback for a series of individual reports submitted over a semester. They found that 92% of first-year students opened their digital feedback at the beginning of a semester, and this declined to 83% for the last piece of work they submitted. Second-year students were less likely to open their feedback. This is probably not inconsistent with the dispiriting findings of a 2004 study in the days of paper submissions, in which 46% of academic staff said that over 20% of the assignments they had marked, with feedback, remained uncollected (Winter & Dye, 2004).

The issue of staff effort in producing feedback is obviously a factor in thinking about this, but getting students to engage with feedback is more important. Zimbardi et al. (2016, p. 641) also looked at the relationship between opening the digital feedback file and grade improvement in subsequent reports, and found that 'the extent to which students interact with their feedback impacts significantly on their performance'. You will also want to consider what feedback is appropriate at what level of the award. For example, you might focus more on the functional and technical aspects of the submission for a first-year submission than is necessary towards the end of a course.

As part of the process of encouraging engagement, the feedback plan should communicate to students what they should do with their feedback and how it is intended to help with subsequent work. Ideally, each unit will include some class time where assessment and feedback are explained before assignment deadlines, followed by some interpretation after work has been handed back. It's also important to encourage students to identify feedback in different contexts and to understand that feedback is not only something written on a sheet handed back with their work, but that it may occur in many teaching and learning situations, all of which may be useful for future assessments.

Timing of feedback

We'd all agree that feedback needs to be timely. This is a handy word that means 'provided when the student will benefit most from it'. It does not mean 'fast'. However, your institution may expect feedback to be supplied at a certain time after submission, in which case you will need to build this into your planning. Look at the types of feedback you've decided to use and estimate how long it will take to provide feedback on each submission, given the number of students. Take into account any technical considerations; you may need time to allocate submissions to different markers and sort out a way of sharing that information, or it may take a while to download or upload large audio or video files, and so on. If it looks as though the logistics will make it likely that some feedback will take an unacceptably long time to produce, or will place an unacceptable strain on individual members of staff, then think about some ways of mitigating the delay, such as:

- Sharing the marking across the team
- Providing some generic feedback to the group after having marked a sample of submissions, which highlights common strengths and weaknesses
- Asking students to carry out a self-assessment so that they review the submission after a short break, so that they continue to think about the assignment
- Using a simpler feedback strategy

There have been some small-scale studies looking at slightly more radical approaches to the timing of feedback. For instance, Phil Race (Race, 2019) has long recommended the separation of marks and feedback, with the feedback being provided several days before the mark. He has also suggested asking students to estimate their mark from the feedback. Jones and Gorra (2013) tried providing limited feedback alongside the grade, and offering more detailed feedback on demand. In general, students tended to request this additional feedback when their grade differed from their expectations. These approaches are intended to encourage student engagement with feedback and develop student agency and self-regulation.

Finally, students need to actually look at the feedback for it to be useful. Mensink and King (2020) found that if the grade was given to students separately from the feedback, which is a common feature of modern learning management systems, 38% of feedback was never accessed. As long ago as 2004, Winter and Dye found that giving the feedback before the mark was considered by students to be the technique most likely to encourage collecting feedback, with a requirement to respond to feedback and compulsory discussion sessions coming a close second and third.

Format of feedback

All of these factors will feed into your decisions about the format of your feedback on a specific task. You need to decide what will be useful and manageable for you and for the student, how much time you would need to prepare the feedback, and how it will be returned to students and accessed by them. In Part 3, there are examples of different types of feedback given on assessment. A longer list, together with an indication of the learning 'pay-off' versus efficiency can be found in Chapter 5 of Phil Race's book, *Making Learning Happen* (Race, 2014). There is no evidence that any one of these formats is more effective than the others. A systematic review of the literature on feedback (Paterson et al., 2020) and a fairly large study of student preferences (Ryan et al., 2019) both showed that multi-modal feedback, that is, using a combination of formats, was generally preferred by students. This might be a combination of annotations and audio, or a checklist plus some personalised comments.

Your strategy could indicate which form of feedback will be used in which situations and give a rough idea of how much might be expected in each case (e.g. a two-minute audio clip, a completed one-page checklist, three points of advice for future work). Your choice will depend on the type of assignment, the stage the student is at in the course; the amount of time you have available, and the resources available to produce the feedback. A checklist might be good for giving instant feedback after a presentation, while annotations and a short, written report might work better for an essay.

Developing your own feedback strategy

How can we convert these ideas about using feedback to develop self-regulation into meaningful action plans for busy teachers and their students?

1. Include the feedback plan in your assignment brief so that expectations are clear from the beginning of the module.
2. Regularly mention the importance of feedback to the learning process and differentiate this from the purpose of justifying the mark.
3. Use formative self, peer, and tutor feedback during the module, to encourage reflection and self-regulation. Try to use questions instead of affirmations or corrections, where possible. With simple factual matters such as mathematical or scientific proofs, you might be saying, 'That's right, and what would happen if...?' With interpretations, you can ask, 'What is the counter-argument?' or, 'What more evidence would you need to change your mind?'. Encourage students to devise these kinds of questions to feedback on what you have said in class; you could offer to provide a response in a future session. Keep reinforcing the idea that feedback is for learning and developing critical thinking more than to prove that your marking is correct.
4. Ask your students questions to encourage early consideration of the value and purpose of the feedback you are going to give them during the course, and during your regular mentions of assessment. You can use a 'one-minute paper' approach for this, and skim through the responses, using them to build some hints into the next teaching session. Questions could include:
   - What did you do with the last assignment feedback you received?
   - What would you like to see in your feedback for this assignment? Be prepared to discuss requests to justify the mark and refer back to the module feedback plan in the assignment brief.
   - What's the most useful feedback you've ever received, in any context?
5. Add a box to the assignment submission/cover sheet, with one or more questions, such as:
   - What did you have most difficulty with?
   - What would you most like me to give feedback on?
   - Is there anything you feel particularly proud of having achieved in this assignment?

This encourages the student to reflect on the process of producing the submission, gives you the chance to focus on something of importance to the student, and further reinforces the separation of marks and feedback.

Moderation strategy

In Chapter 2, we introduced moderation as a collection of processes which aim to ensure consistency and standards. While Bloxham et al. (2015) identified various activities which had been labelled as moderation, we will only use the processes based on the practice of more than one teacher reviewing the same student submission, using the same assignment brief and marking rubric, and then comparing their judgements and suggested feedback. This is moderation as consensus-seeking activity, as Sadler (2013) describes it.

There may be a requirement to carry out moderation in your university and/or country, and the processes may be clearly defined for you, or you may have freedom to make your own decisions. Moderation is an important component of processes to reduce uncertainty in making judgements, and so I recommend that you build it in to your planning, whatever the external requirements. The principal aim of moderation is to ensure that marking is as fair, accurate, and consistent as possible, but an important secondary aim is to develop shared understandings of assessment among teachers, so it is important to keep both these purposes in mind when planning the processes. You might choose, or be asked to use, one or more of the following approaches to moderation.

Pre-marking calibration

A calibration activity is one in which a group of teachers all mark the same assignment or small set of assignments, and then compare their grades and notes on feedback. They are designed to build confidence in the consistency of marking and feedback across the team, shared understanding of marking rubrics and feedback expectations, as well as providing reference points for comparison of standards. Calibration can be used if you have many markers grading the same assessment task, but it is equally effective for small teams marking many assessments between them. These activities can be very confidence-building for novice markers, as they give an opportunity to share ideas, questions, and concerns before they are launched into full judgement mode with a pile of submissions to mark. They are also very useful if many people are marking a task which shares an assignment brief, but where students have chosen very different topics to focus on, such as a project or dissertation.

The timing of the activity depends on the main purpose. You can use calibration to test out a new marking rubric, or familiarise a team of teachers with the expectations of an assignment brief, before teaching starts. In that situation you need access to previous similar assignments. However, you are most likely to use it just before marking starts in earnest, to provide a check-in on expectations and standards.

The basic process is to select one or two assignments from the submissions at random, anonymise if possible, and distribute to all markers, along with the assignment brief, marking criteria, and feedback sheet. Teachers mark each submission and decide on a grade and some feedback in line with your usual expectations. If possible, collate the marks and feedback and share the anonymised data with colleagues, although you can just discuss it without anonymising if you prefer. You can then discuss the outcomes. You may want to talk about:

- The range of marks (it is always surprisingly large – don't dwell on any angst about this).
- What the feedback focused on: was it related to the marking criteria? Did it reflect the grade given?
- Were there any words in the criteria which led people down a particular decision-making path? If so, could you discuss perceived meaning and the importance of them? Possible candidates might be words like 'analyse' or 'interpret' or 'advanced'.
- Whether people might be persuaded to change their marks or feedback as a result of the discussion.

After the meeting, colleagues can continue with their marking. Encourage a continued discussion about the interpretation of the criteria if colleagues encounter any uncertainty. Sometimes, just explaining to someone else why you are having difficulty making a decision can help in unblocking the decision.

Independent second marking

This method is usually applied to a sample of work, where the **moderator** marks a sample of work independently, using the assignment brief and criteria available to the first marker. You will need to make a decision during planning about how to identify the sample. Will it be based on a certain number, or percentage, of submissions from each grade band? A number from each different marker, where there was more than one person grading the work? Everything which failed? Everything which got the top mark? These decisions will be based on a number of factors, such as the number and experience of the markers, the time available to the first and second markers, the complexity of the assignment, and any variations in grading in previous years with the same or a similar assignment. You also need to decide, at this planning stage, when moderation can begin. Must it happen after all of the first marking has been completed, or can it start once a suitable sample size is available?

Joint second marking

This kind of second marking is most usual for an ephemeral piece of student work, such as a presentation or performance. Markers may work together on their judgements, discussing their interpretation of the marking rubric and possible feedback points as they go, or they can work independently and then compare their judgements before agreeing a final grade and feedback. Their post-marking discussion will be similar to the pre-marking calibration.

Review of a sample of submissions and grades

This is the most common approach in the UK, and is focused on consistency and fairness in the application of marking criteria and provision of feedback. The moderator will usually see a sample of work alongside the marks and feedback. They do not re-mark the work, but rather skim over the key parts of the submission to see how the rubrics have been applied. Decisions about sampling are similar to those for second marking.

Review of grades

A review of grades usually involves a statistical comparison of the marks for one assignment task with those for other modules, or for the same task in previous years. This approach is commonly used in large public examinations such as entrance tests or national school examinations, to even out differences between markers and normalise the distribution of grades from year to year, so that roughly the same number of students achieve in each grade band each year. It is problematic in higher education, because cohort sizes are usually too small for significant comparisons, and small changes in context may have a strong effect, and because assessment is intended to be standards-based, so that statistical normalisation may not reflect individual achievements. However, keeping an eye on marks profiles can be useful to identify situations where further moderation would be useful. Are there more failures or high grades than usual? Did the same cohort of students perform significantly better, or worse, on the average than on another of their modules? These are useful data to discuss in a programme team.

External examining

External examining is a form of moderation that is carried out by a person who is not employed at the same institution. This person is usually a teacher in the same subject, who is provided with information about assessment practices at the institution where they are examining, as well as with a sample of work, marks, and feedback in the same way as the review of the sample described for internal moderation. While internal moderation is focused on individual tasks, the external examiner is likely to look at a range of modules, which enables a review of standards and their interpretation across a programme team. They should give general feedback on the standards of student achievement and marking on the programme, compared to other programmes with which they are familiar.

Conclusion

Marking and feedback are complex processes that require you and your colleagues to make judgements which affect students' future academic and professional careers. Detailed planning will improve the reliability of these processes and help you to manage your time more effectively.

Further reading

The EAT framework (Evans, 2016) brings together a lot of the research on feedback into a detailed strategy and is well worth a look, especially if you are looking at feedback from a programme-level perspective.

The limitations of internal and external moderation respectively are discussed in Bloxham (2009) and Bloxham, Hudson et al. (2015).

For case studies of innovative assessment alongside a theoretical interpretation, see Carless (2015).

References

Ahmed Shafi, A., Hatley, J., Middleton, T., Millican, R., & Templeton, S. (2017). The role of assessment feedback in developing academic buoyancy. *Assessment & Evaluation in Higher Education*, 1–13. https://doi.org/10.1080/02602938.2017.1356265

Ajjawi, R., Kent, F., Broadbent, J., Tai, J. H.-M., Bearman, M., & Boud, D. (2021). Feedback that works: A realist review of feedback interventions for written tasks. *Studies in Higher Education*, 1–14. https://doi.org/10.1080/03075079.2021.1894115

Anderson, L. W., & Krathwohl, D. R. (Eds.). (2001). *A taxonomy for learning, teaching and assessing: A revision of Bloom's Taxonomy of educational objectives: Complete edition*. New York: Longman.

Biggs, J. B., & Collis, K. F. (1982). *Evaluating the quality of learning: The SOLO taxonomy (Structure of the Observed Learning Outcome)*. New York: Academic Press.

Blair, A., Wyburn-Powell, A., Goodwin, M., & Shields, S. (2014). Can dialogue help to improve feedback on examinations? *Studies in Higher Education*, 39(6), 1039–1054. https://doi.org/10.1080/03075079.2013.777404

Bloom, B. (1956). *Taxonomy of educational objectives: The classification of educational goals*. Chicago, IL: Susan Fauer Company.

Bloxham, S. (2009). Marking and moderation in the UK: False assumptions and wasted resources. *Assessment & Evaluation in Higher Education*, 34(2), 209–220. https://doi.org/10.1080/02602930801955978

Bloxham, S., & Boyd, P. (2007). *Developing effective assessment in higher education: A practical guide*. Maidenhead: Open University Press/McGraw Hill.

Bloxham, S., Boyd, P., & Orr, S. (2011). Mark my words: The role of assessment criteria in UK higher education grading practices. *Studies in Higher Education*, 36(6), 655–670. https://doi.org/10.1080/03075071003777716

Bloxham, S., Hudson, J., den Outer, B. and Price, M. (2015). External peer review of assessment: An effective approach to verifying standards? *Higher Education Research & Development*, 34(6), 1069–1082. https://doi.org/10.1080/07294360.2015.1024629

Bloxham, S., Hughes, C., & Adie, L. (2015). What's the point of moderation? A discussion of the purposes achieved through contemporary moderation practices. *Assessment & Evaluation in Higher Education*, 1–16. https://doi.org/10.1080/02602938.2015.1039932

Boud, D., & Molloy, E. (2012). Rethinking models of feedback for learning: The challenge of design. *Assessment & Evaluation in Higher Education*, 38(6), 698–712. https://doi.org/10.1080/02602938.2012.691462

Carless, D. (2015). *Excellence in university assessment: Learning from award-winning practice*. London: Routledge.

Carless, D., & Chan, K. K. H. (2016). Managing dialogic use of exemplars. *Assessment & Evaluation in Higher Education*, 1–12. https://doi.org/10.1080/02602938.2016.1211246

Chan, Z., & Ho, S. (2019). Good and bad practices in rubrics: The perspectives of students and educators. *Assessment & Evaluation in Higher Education*, 44(4), 533–545. https://doi.org/10.1080/02602938.2018.1522528

Cullen, R., Forsyth, R., Ringan, N., Gregory, S., & Roche, M. (2016). Developing and using marking rubrics based on the MMU standard. *Learning*, 11(2), 75–92.

Dawson, P. (2017). Assessment rubrics: Towards clearer and more replicable design, research and practice. *Assessment & Evaluation in Higher Education*, 42(3), 347–360. https://doi.org/10.1080/02602938.2015.1111294

Dawson, P., Henderson, M., Mahoney, P., Phillips, M., Ryan, T., Boud, D., & Molloy, E. (2018). What makes for effective feedback: Staff and student perspectives. *Assessment & Evaluation in Higher Education*, 1–12. https://doi.org/10.1080/02602938.2018.1467877

Evans, C. (2016). *Enhancing assessment feedback practice in higher education: The EAT framework*. Southampton: University of Southampton. Available online at: https://eatframework.org. uk.

Forsythe, A., & Johnson, S. (2016). Thanks, but no-thanks for the feedback. *Assessment & Evaluation in Higher Education*, 1–10. https://doi.org/10.1080/02602938.2016.1202190

Hill, J., & West, H. (2020). Improving the student learning experience through dialogic feed-forward assessment. *Assessment & Evaluation in Higher Education*, 45(1), 82–97. https://doi.org/10.1080/02602938.2019.1608908

Jones, O., & Gorra, A. (2013). Assessment feedback only on demand: Supporting the few not supplying the many. *Active Learning in Higher Education*, 14(2), 149–161. https://doi.org/10.1177/1469787413481131

Kite, J., & Phongsavan, P. (2016). Evaluating standards-based assessment rubrics in a postgraduate public health subject. *Assessment & Evaluation in Higher Education*, 1–13. https://doi.org/10.1080/02602938.2016.1199773

Knight, P. T., & Yorke, M. (2003). *Assessment, Learning and Employability*. SRHE/OUP.

Matshedisho, K. R. (2019). Straddling rows and columns: Students' (mis)conceptions of an assessment rubric. *Assessment & Evaluation in Higher Education*, 1–11. https://doi.org/10.1080/02602938.2019.1616671

Mensink, P. J., & King, K. (2020). Student access of online feedback is modified by the availability of assessment marks, gender and academic performance. *British Journal of Educational Technology*, 51(1), 10–22. https://doi.org/https://doi.org/10.1111/bjet.12752

Nicol, D. (2010). From monologue to dialogue: Improving written feedback processes in mass higher education. *Assessment & Evaluation in Higher Education*, 35(5), 501–517. https://doi.org/10.1080/02602931003786559

Nicol, D., & Macfarlane-Dick, D. (2006). Formative assessment and self-regulated learning: A model and seven principles of good feedback practice. *Studies in Higher Education*, 31(2), 199–218. http://dx.doi.org/10.1080/03075070600572090

O'Donovan, B. M., den Outer, B., Price, M., & Lloyd, A. (2021). What makes good feedback good? *Studies in Higher Education*, 46(2), 318–329. https://doi.org/10.1080/03075079.2019.1630812

Paterson, C., Paterson, N., Jackson, W., & Work, F. (2020). What are students' needs and preferences for academic feedback in higher education? A systematic review. *Nurse Education Today*, 85, 104236. https://doi.org/https://doi.org/10.1016/j.nedt.2019.104236

Pitt, E., & Norton, L. (2016). 'Now that's the feedback I want!' Students' reactions to feedback on graded work and what they do with it. *Assessment & Evaluation in Higher Education*, 1–18. https://doi.org/10.1080/02602938.2016.1142500

Price, M., Handley, K., Millar, J., & O'Donovan, B. (2010). Feedback: All that effort, but what is the effect? *Assessment & Evaluation in Higher Education, 35*(3), 277–289. https://doi.org/10.1080/02602930903541007

Race, P. (2014). *Making learning happen: A guide for post-compulsory education.* London: Sage.

Race, P. (2019). *The lecturer's toolkit: A practical guide to assessment, learning and teaching* (5th ed.). Abingdon: Routledge.

Rublee, M. R. (2014). Rubrics in the political science classroom: Packing a serious analytical punch. *PS: Political Science & Politics, 47*(01), 199–203. https://doi.org/doi:10.1017/S1049096513001704

Rust, C. (2002). The impact of assessment on student learning: How can the research literature practically help to inform the development of departmental assessment strategies and learner-centred assessment practices? *Active Learning in Higher Education, 3*(2), 145–158. http://alh.sagepub.com/cgi/content/abstract/3/2/145

Ryan, T., Henderson, M., & Phillips, M. (2019). Feedback modes matter: Comparing student perceptions of digital and non-digital feedback modes in higher education. *British Journal of Educational Technology, 50*(3), 1507–1523. https://doi.org/https://doi.org/10.1111/bjet.12749

Sadler, D. R. (2013). Assuring academic achievement standards: From moderation to calibration. *Assessment in Education: Principles, Policy & Practice, 20*(1), 5–19. https://doi.org/10.1080/0969594X.2012.714742

Shields, S. (2015). 'My work is bleeding': Exploring students' emotional responses to first-year assignment feedback. *Teaching in Higher Education, 20*(6), 614–624. https://doi.org/10.1080/13562517.2015.1052786

Williams, J., Kane, D., Sagu, S., & Smith, E. (2008). *Exploring the national student survey: Assessment and feedback issues.* London: The Higher Education Academy, Centre for Research into Quality.

Winstone, N. E., & Carless, D. (2021). Who is feedback for? The influence of accountability and quality assurance agendas on the enactment of feedback processes. *Assessment in Education: Principles, Policy & Practice,* 1–18. https://doi.org/10.1080/0969594X.2021.1926221

Winstone, N. E., Nash, R. A., Rowntree, J., & Parker, M. (2017). 'It'd be useful, but I wouldn't use it': Barriers to university students' feedback seeking and recipience. *Studies in Higher Education, 42*(11), 2026–2041. https://doi.org/10.1080/03075079.2015.1130032

Winter, C., & Dye, V. (2004). *An investigation into the reasons why students do not collect marked assignments and the accompanying feedback.* http://wlv.openrepository.com/wlv/bitstream/2436/3780/1/An%20investigation%20pgs%20133–141.pdf

Zimbardi, K., Colthorpe, K., Dekker, A., Engstrom, C., Bugarcic, A., Worthy, P., Victor, R., Chunduri, P., Lluka, L., & Long, P. (2016). Are they using my feedback? The extent of students' feedback use has a large impact on subsequent academic performance. *Assessment & Evaluation in Higher Education,* 1–20. https://doi.org/10.1080/02602938.2016.1174187

7

TEACHING FOR EFFECTIVE ASSESSMENT

Chapter overview

This chapter explores:

- Preparing students for assessment
- Managing formative assessment
- The role of peer and self-assessment
- Supporting group assessment effectively

Introduction

You might think we've spent a long time thinking about the design of the assessment, when most of your time with students will actually be spent on teaching. The reason is that assessment and teaching are intertwined. Many of us would agree with the quote from Boud (1995, p. 35), which appears in every book about assessment: 'Students can, with difficulty, escape from the effects of poor teaching, they cannot (by definition if they want to graduate) escape the effects of poor assessment.' You could reverse this context to say that a badly designed assessment will make a course difficult to teach.

For all of the reasons we considered in Chapter 1, assessment is important throughout a course of study, and the teaching needs to be aligned to the eventual goal of successful completion of the assessment. This isn't to say that the whole module or course needs to be fixated on the assignment, that you should be spoon-feeding students with a perfect model for the task, or that it isn't possible to go off in different directions and take a more creative approach. You are just acknowledging that students will be concerned with the assignment, that they are likely to do better if they start preparing for it earlier, and that focusing on getting the students to the task will give you a good structure for planning your teaching. In this chapter, we will look at how you can incorporate planning for the assignment naturally into your teaching and make best use of the time you have available with the students. We will focus on assessment; for some good, basic course planning advice which covers a wider range of activities, see the further reading suggestions at the end of the chapter.

The assignment brief

All that time spent thinking about the assignment brief will have been well spent, but don't assume that students will automatically pore over it without your bringing it explicitly to their attention. Introduce it in the first session, explaining what you are all working towards and how you are going to support them towards successful submission. Give them a rough idea of how you expect them to prepare their assignments, without getting into too much detail at this stage.

During the module, you can highlight ideas, current events, or examples which might be useful to follow up as they think about their submissions. Make suggestions about where students could be up to with their assignment planning at regular intervals, without making them feel anxious about their own progress. This is a difficult balance, of course: use phrases like, 'If you haven't already made notes on about five papers, then I'd suggest you set yourself a target of getting one done a day for the next few days; you'll find it will really help to set yourself small tasks'; 'It's not too late to interview a couple of your peers about their attitude to X'; 'Sam's question is going to be really useful to anyone who is working on this particular option; does anyone else have a related question?'. These regular prompts will remind students to get on, and reassure those who get started early and then worry they may be on the wrong track. You can normalise discussion about the assessment throughout the module, showing the links between what you are teaching and their own work. This connection is very obvious to the teacher, but may be less so to a student. A video explainer of the assignment brief is also a very useful reference point for students, something they can refer back to as they are working on their submissions, and can head off a lot of repeated questions (Gellen et al., 2020).

Talking about assessment

Micari and Calkins (2019) found that a perception of teacher openness and students' own approaches to help-seeking in class were correlated to grades, indicating that it is important to normalise talking about assessment and potential challenges students may have. You can encourage this by building discussion about the assessment into every session, and suggesting how students can get started and move on with their assignment work. When you are planning teaching, make reference to the assignment task every time you work with students. This doesn't need to be a restrictive condition on your planning or session structures; it is just a matter of making regular reference to it, so that students know that the assignment is embedded in the module and that you are open to discussing it throughout the course.

Designing formative assessment

When we defined formative assessment in Chapter 1, we simply said it was assessment that didn't count for grades. This is more accurately a statement of what it is not than a definition, of course; an accurate definition needs many more words. Black and Wiliam (2009) developed a definition based on the notion of 'contingent moments', which cover a broad range of teaching activities:

> Practice in a classroom is formative to the extent that evidence about student achievement is elicited, interpreted, and used by teachers, learners, or their peers, to make decisions about the next steps in instruction that are likely to be better, or better founded, than the decisions they would have taken in the absence of the evidence that was elicited. (Black & Wiliam, 2009, p. 9)

A review of the literature by Clark (2012) linked formative assessment very strongly to the development of self-regulation in students, underlining its importance in skills development as well as preparation for summative assessment.

In the context of a module or programme, a simple way of thinking about formative work is as activities which students complete to help them to prepare for summative assessment, and on which they receive feedback. These activities are designed and integrated into the teaching of the course.

Formative assessment can be used for many of the purposes listed in Chapter 1: you and your students can use it to judge students' knowledge, competence, and progress towards the final summative assessment, to identify areas for development, and to build student confidence in their ability to achieve the module learning outcomes. If the group of students is small enough for you to compare their previous draft or other work with a current piece, you can use ipsative approaches to show where they have improved. For larger groups, you can encourage them to make comparative judgements of their own on their improvements.

Because formative assessment doesn't contribute to a student's final grade, you should have more flexibility over how you design it than for summative assessment, which is of necessity bounded by regulations and quality assurance processes. Formative activities might be carried out in timetabled sessions, or as independent or group study outside class; you can give feedback verbally as activities are happening, or ask for work to be submitted for you to look at, or you can support the use of peer feedback on student progress. You might use formative assessment as a chance to try out things which you'd like to use in summative assessment, but don't yet dare to let loose in a more conventional structure.

The disadvantage of the fact that it doesn't count to the final qualification is that students may not prioritise engagement with formative assessment. To make the best use of everyone's time, it is important to design activity that both you and the students can manage and that adds value to the preparation for summative assessment. The four key questions of validity, manageability, clarity, and satisfaction remain a good guide for planning formative activities, with some modifications:

1   Validity: will completion contribute to preparation for the final assignment? You don't need to cover all of the learning outcomes for the module for every activity.
2   Manageability: can the time needed to explain, support, collect, and give feedback be incorporated into the time you have available for teaching the module, and not add to your workload?
3   Clarity: will students understand what is expected and how it relates to the final assignment, so that they see the value of engaging with it?
4   Satisfaction: will I be able to use the outcomes of the activity to adapt the remaining teaching on the module?

The rest of this section offers some ideas for ways you might design and manage formative assessment, taking these questions into account.

Dialogue

The simplest form of formative assessment is to engage students in dialogue during the course. This can be in real time, during classes or tutorials, or asynchronously using digital communications tools (email or online discussion software). It can be one to one between teacher and student, or within a group, or between the group and the teacher. The important factor is that questions are asked and answered.

You might ask a question in class which is answered by a student, and you provide feedback by responding to them. It might be a question that has a 'correct' answer, which restricts your feedback to either 'Yes, that's right' or 'I can see why you might have said that, but it's not the answer I was looking for'. It might be an open question related to the topic: 'Has anyone ever lived in a country where monetary policy favours high interest rates?' or 'What policies at a social media company might lead to advertising revenue being prioritised over child safety?', where the aim is to have a discussion and relate it to the class content and the eventual assessment tasks. Dialogue might also be generated by a student asking you a question; instead of answering it directly, you can ask other students what they think the response should be.

As the teacher using dialogue as formative assessment, your role is to facilitate the conversation and keep it focused on the assessment task. You will be able to make those connections much better than the students.

The outline

Asking students to provide a plan for a final coursework submission is a good way to see if they are on track. This could be the outline of a piece of written work, presentation, or timed production such as a play or a poetry reading, or a sketch of a final product, for example. Such work is fairly quick to review, and you may be able to see any obvious gaps and suggest further reading to improve the work without spending too much time per student.

Producing an outline is useful preparation for both a coursework submission and an examination. For an unseen examination, you can give the students an example question and ask them to produce an outline, giving them an opportunity to develop their skills in planning answers in examination conditions. For a seen examination, where the questions are provided in advance, your feedback on an outline may mean that the students go into the time-pressured environment with more confidence.

Requesting an outline also provides a cue for students to stage their work over the course. You need to think about how to encourage students to complete and submit an outline at a time that will be useful to them.

Reflection on progress

As an alternative, or a follow-up, to the production of an outline, you can ask students to write a paragraph about where they are up to in relation to completion of the assignment and how they perceive their current successes and challenges. You can ask them to use a simple reflective model such as Gibbs' (1988) or Rolfe's (2002) to provide a consistent structure. A reflection gives you a snapshot of where they are up to and the opportunity to make some suggestions about process, such as signposting to a librarian or writing skills service if you have them, or moving on now to focus on a different part of the assignment.

This type of formative assessment isn't appropriate in all situations. Unless they are used to reflection, some students may find this kind of activity quite difficult to do, distracting them from the main task of assignment preparation. Also, it won't give you a clear idea of how much content they have managed to consider, so you may see a very good reflection on progress, on which you make encouraging remarks, only to find that the final submission has completely missed the point. A reflection is best used when students are experienced learners who are used to thinking about how they go about academic work as well as what they are studying.

The draft

Formative assessment can be a shortened version of the final summative assessment, or even a full draft. This is a common approach for large projects or dissertations, when a supervisor might give feedback on individual chapters. This model works well when the number of students per supervisor is relatively small, and when the supervisor has specialist knowledge which speeds up the analysis of the work provided.

Reviewing drafts is unlikely to be manageable for a large class. I am aware of some unpublished work where people have tried giving detailed feedback on a draft, but then didn't give feedback on the final piece of work, just a grade. The work of providing feedback is thus shifted to an earlier part of the course. This may be a risky strategy in some university contexts: students would need to understand that their only opportunity for feedback is on the draft, and colleagues, and external examiners if you have them, need to support the approach if it is contrary to usual university expectations. It may also be impossible to find the time to provide this kind of feedback during periods of the year that are allocated for teaching. Remember that your plans need to be manageable.

Paragraphs or examples

Where reading a full draft or looking at a final piece of artwork for every student is impossible, you could ask students to prepare a complete section of their submission. It could be an abstract, an introduction, a conclusion, a scene in a play, the methods section of a laboratory report, or whatever small section could be produced as a coherent whole to show how the student can put together ideas. You can use extracts from your marking criteria to generate simple feedback, accommodating the fact that you aren't looking at a whole piece. If one criterion was 'Links between theory and practice are identified' (see Table 6.3) and the sample simply mentions practice, you could ask the question 'What theory do you think underpins this example?'. The theory might be better placed in a part of the submission you haven't yet seen; this kind of question just signals that it will be needed to complete the work. You don't need to provide all the answers for students; asking questions should be sufficient at this stage (see Boud & Molloy, 2012).

There may be some drawbacks to this approach, so asking for a sample won't work in all situations. It can be difficult to isolate a small section of a complete piece in a meaningful way, making both the production of this sample and the generation of feedback a pointless exercise.

Regular tasks

It makes sense to encourage students to work towards their summative assignment all the way through the module. This gives them time to test ideas out, find a good range of literature, try new practical techniques, and so on. There are a few exceptions to this situation: perhaps you give out a list of essay titles or practical activities at the beginning of the term and then cover each topic weekly, so that they can't really get started until you have covered their topic of choice. However, in most courses it makes sense for students to tackle their assignment in stages.

You can help them to structure their preparation for the assignment by setting regular tasks that build towards their final submission. You can then set aside class time to discuss progress. You may also be lucky enough have access to student support services, which can provide specialist study skills related to the activity, such as library searches, writing skills, or using statistics packages.

For an essay, you could consider some of the tasks in Table 7.1.

Table 7.1 Regular tasks to help students work towards an essay

Task	Description
Choose a title	Pick one of the titles, or write your own, and write down five reasons why you want to write about it
Start the literature search	Find one relevant paper and write a synopsis which links it to your chosen title
Plan	Write an outline for the essay
Abstract	Write a summary of your arguments in 250 words

If it is manageable, you could scan over these tasks and give brief feedback. This can be done in class, if students are working independently during the session, or by asking them to submit electronically to you by email or using digital submission tools that are included in most Virtual Learning Environments used in universities. These tools make it easier to comment directly on a piece of work and return it to the student; email attachments usually require more administration time, but of course it depends on your personal preference.

If you have large student numbers, then reviewing every student's task may not be manageable. You can still suggest regular tasks and use other ways to check in. See the section below on self- and peer assessment for some ways of supporting students to review tasks themselves.

Regular tasks may also be a way for students to build up a portfolio. For a competence portfolio, students need to show that they can carry out a range of activities to a certain standard, so these are likely to be completed all through the module. These can be laboratory clinical, or practical skills, or computing techniques, for instance. In this situation, a teacher or designated assessor will often need to sign off successful completion, so the time needed for this needs to be factored into your teaching schedule.

For a synthesis portfolio, you might be expecting students to carry out a series of tasks and then create a summary to show how the tasks are linked, or what they have learned from the process of carrying out the work. You can think about looking at a sample of their tasks, or encourage them to use self- and peer assessment to review each other's progress.

As these kinds of portfolio tasks will contribute to the final assignment, you need to be careful about giving feedback that guides students' development, rather than making corrections that could make the work more like yours than their own. Asking questions in formative feedback is a good strategy; some examples are given in Table 7.2.

Table 7.2 Examples of questions for formative feedback

Have you thought about?
What would [insert author of your choice] say?
Where will this argument go next?
When you show this to a fellow student, do they understand it?
Could you make this paragraph more concise?
Can you review what we did in week 3?

Tests

A low-pressure test can break up the teaching in a fun way, as well as giving you and the students a sense of where they are up to in the course. Tests or quizzes are a good way of checking knowledge and letting you and the students know where there are any gaps that may need to be reviewed before the final assessment. They are also important preparation for examinations that will use a similar type of question. The most efficient way to offer a test is to use computer-marked multiple-choice questions, but your choice should depend on what you want to achieve. If you want to provoke discussion about questions and answers, you may consider a paper-based quiz where the students swap answer sheets and grade each other's responses, followed by a conversation in their pairs.

You can also encourage discussion by using an online app or web-based tool in which students respond to on-screen questions in real time, using their own mobile devices or computers. If they don't all have an appropriate device, you can suggest they work in pairs or threes, where one person has a phone or computer, and they all agree a response. You'll need to allow a bit more time for the answers in that situation, but it is an approach that encourages discussion and group work, so you may want to try it even if the students do have their own devices.

These apps work best with multiple-choice questions, or asking students to type in one or two words. If students identify themselves by name in the app, you can use these tools to review individual progress. It's probably best not to share individual scores in class, as this is quite exposing for students, unless you have a small group with high levels of trust. However, the apps also usually give you the number of people who have chosen each response, so you can use this feature to consider each possible choice, and talk about why people may have picked a particular answer. You can round up the discussion by making general suggestions for further work to improve scores for next time or pointing out common errors.

Self- and peer assessment

Students need to learn what is expected in a higher education course and adapt their own work to achieve the grades they are seeking. Some of this learning will come from what you say about assessment while you are teaching, your well-written assignment brief, and your feedback on formative activities. As Panadero et al. (2018) point out, this is a teacher-centred approach to assessment. This focus can be hard to shift; in relation to summative assessment, the university teacher holds a great deal of power, and because of this a student may find it hard to question your pronouncements, or to trust their own judgements about the tasks you set.

The use of peer and self-assessment may help students to develop their own ability to interpret your expectations and to learn to self-regulate their own learning (Cassidy, 2011; Kirby & Downs, 2007). Some of these benefits are thought to come from the development of extended dialogue about assessment and the consequent improvement in student assessment literacy (Carless, 2019; Carless & Boud, 2018). Much of the research on self- and peer assessment focuses on the accuracy of students giving grades, which is quite variable, and may be affected by gender and power dynamics (Boud et al., 2014; Langan et al., 2008), but the techniques can be used without being concerned with marks. Adachi et al. (2017, p. 295) use these simple definitions of self- and peer assessment:

Self assessment: students judge and make decisions about their own work against particular criteria.

Peer assessment: students judge and make decisions about the work of their peers against particular criteria.

Both approaches are thus about making judgements, which is an important competence for both self-regulation and for future professional work. Self-assessment can be added to your formative assessment activities by providing prompt questions like the ones in Table 7.3. The reflection on progress activity already encourages self-reflection, which can be developed further by using some of these questions.

Table 7.3 Example of questions to prompt self-assessment

How do you think your work is going?

Which aspects of the question have you covered?

How does this draft/extract meet the learning outcomes?

If you were giving yourself feedback, what would you say about this piece of work?

What grade do you think this is worth? Why?

Peer assessment adds the dimension of providing constructive feedback to another person, which is an important element of team work, so including peer judgements may be an additional benefit if one of your programme's learning outcomes includes the ability to work effectively in a team.

Most of the approaches to formative assessment mentioned above can be used to gain peer feedback as well as, or instead of, teacher feedback. In class, students can exchange abstracts, paragraphs, or other parts of work in progress. In the earlier years of higher education, they can begin by having a discussion about process, using questions such as, 'Where did you start with this?' or, 'What do you want the reader (or viewer, or listener) to take away?'. As they develop confidence and skills in making judgements, they can use a simplified form of the assignment marking criteria to provide feedback on each other's work.

It is important to manage peer assessment actively; Sridharan and Boud (2019) found that peer assessment can be ineffective or even detrimental if they are not introduced and supported properly. One example of this is criticisms, or 'crits', which are often used in schools of art: a student presents an artefact or some ideas to their teacher and other students, who then provide some feedback publicly. There are some obvious drawbacks to this for students who find public feedback difficult to receive and if criticism appears to be of the student rather than of the piece of work (Jones, 1996). However, the argument for using them regularly is that it is useful to experience this in the safe environment of supportive tutors and peers before presenting their work to a less tactful public. As the teacher, you need to ensure that critique is constructive and provides guidance for improvement, and focuses on the work, not the person. As with group work, it is sensible to develop ground rules with the cohort before beginning the process, including a discussion of how to present feedback and how you will manage the discussion to keep it productive.

Exemplars

An assignment exemplar is an artefact that demonstrates to students what the teacher is looking for in the task. This could be work from a previous cohort (used with permission) or an example constructed by the teacher. It is possible to use exemplars of different standards, to show the difference between grade bands. In my experience, students very often ask for exemplars, but they should be used with caution. Bell et al. (2013) found in a survey that students who were already self-regulating, with high assessment literacy, were worried that, if they were creative and didn't produce something like the exemplar, they would be penalised, and students who were dependent on the teacher and wanted precise guidance asked for more and more exemplars. Handley and Williams (2011) suggest that excerpts may be useful for discussion in class about criteria and expectations rather than full exemplars, and that they can also be used for the same purpose among tutors, if many are teaching towards the same assignment task.

To et al. (2021) carried out a systematic review of the use of exemplars and concluded that they are particularly effective if they are used by students in peer review after the completion of a first draft of the assignment. A smaller review by Carter et al. (2018) found that exemplar activities increased student engagement and participation in class.

Supporting group assessment

In Chapter 5, we considered suitable assessment tasks for group work and ways to set up the groups. During the course, you will almost certainly need to support the process of group working as much as guiding them towards the production of the submission. It will help to set out clear ground rules at the beginning of the course; these are likely to have more impact if you discuss and agree them with the whole cohort of students. In such discussions, you can also emphasise the transferability of effective group membership to future work or life plans. Table 7.4 has some factors you and the students should consider in thinking about process.

Table 7.4 Group work protocols

Selection of a method of communication	How will group members contact each other and share documents?
Frequency of contact	How often should each group member check in to update colleagues on progress outside meetings?
Frequency and length of meetings	How often should the group check in together, whether it is in person or online, and how long should meetings be?
Allocation of tasks	Who will do what, and by when? Include process-related activities such as scheduling meetings, and taking and sharing notes.
Managing changes	How will individuals let other group members know about suggested changes to agreed tasks, an unavoidable absence and ways to mitigate it, progress or lack of it on a given task?
Concerns about process or contributions	How will individuals raise concerns to the group, and what actions might be taken? When should concerns be escalated to the tutor? What is expected of the tutor in this situation?

Clear ground rules will help to avoid small problems escalating to disputes which you will be asked to arbitrate. You also need to have a plan in place for managing situations where a group really can't work together effectively, or if something comes up which means that one or more members of the group can no longer contribute, for instance due to illness, or a breakdown of the group relationships. If any of these situations happens, you will need to adapt the group assignment to make it manageable for a smaller number and to set an alternative smaller task for the individual(s) who can no longer participate with the group. We considered the choice of an alternative task in Chapter 5, as it will of course depend on the original group task. You may not need to use these contingency plans, but it's a good idea to have them ready.

Conclusion

It is important to embed assessment in your teaching and to make regular and relevant links between other aspects of the module and the final, summative assessment task. The creation of a concise, clear assignment brief is key, and should be accompanied with frequent invitations to consider how each part of the course relates to the assignment, prompts to get on with the work, and opportunities to discuss and share progress with you and with peers. Staging the development of the assignment with formative activities will build student confidence and also give you a sense of how things are going and whether you need to reinforce any areas where there seems to be misunderstanding or confusion.

Further reading

You will find useful information about linking teaching and assessment in Race (2019) and Bale and Seabrook (2021).

References

Adachi, C., Tai, J. H.-M., & Dawson, P. (2017). Academics' perceptions of the benefits and challenges of self and peer assessment in higher education. *Assessment & Evaluation in Higher Education*, 1–13. https://doi.org/10.1080/02602938.2017.1339775

Bale, R., & Seabrook, M. (2021). *Introduction to university teaching*. London: Sage.

Bell, A., Mladenovic, R., & Price, M. (2013). Students' perceptions of the usefulness of marking guides, grade descriptors and annotated exemplars. *Assessment & Evaluation in Higher Education*, 38(7), 769–788. https://doi.org/10.1080/02602938.2012.714738

Black, P., & Wiliam, D. (2009). Developing the theory of formative assessment. *Educational Assessment, Evaluation and Accountability* (formerly: *Journal of Personnel Evaluation in Education*), 21(1), 5.

Boud, D. (1995). Assessment and learning: Contradictory or complementary? In P. Knight (Ed.), *Assessment for learning in higher education* (pp. 35–48). London: Kogan Page.

Boud, D., Lawson, R., & Thompson, D. G. (2014). The calibration of student judgement through self-assessment: Disruptive effects of assessment patterns. *Higher Education Research & Development*, *34*(1), 45–59. https://doi.org/10.1080/07294360.2014.934328

Boud, D., & Molloy, E. (2012). Rethinking models of feedback for learning: The challenge of design. *Assessment & Evaluation in Higher Education*, *38*(6), 698–712. https://doi.org/1 0.1080/02602938.2012.691462

Carless, D. (2019). Feedback loops and the longer-term: Towards feedback spirals. *Assessment & Evaluation in Higher Education*, *44*(5), 705–714. https://doi.org/10.1080/02 602938.2018.1531108

Carless, D., & Boud, D. (2018). The development of student feedback literacy: Enabling uptake of feedback. *Assessment & Evaluation in Higher Education*, 1315–1325. https:// doi.org/10.1080/02602938.2018.1463354

Carter, R., Salamonson, Y., Ramjan, L. M., & Halcomb, E. (2018). Students' use of exemplars to support academic writing in higher education: An integrative review. *Nurse Education Today*, *65*, 87–93. https://doi.org/https://doi.org/10.1016/j. nedt.2018.02.038

Cassidy, S. (2011). Self-regulated learning in higher education: Identifying key component processes. *Studies in Higher Education*, *36*(8), 989–1000. https://doi.org/10.1080/030750 79.2010.503269

Clark, I. (2012). Formative assessment: Assessment is for self-regulated learning. *Educational Psychology Review*, *24*(2), 205–249. https://doi.org/10.1007/s10648-011- 9191-6

Gellen, S., Saunders, F., Stannard, J., McAllister-Gibson, C., & Simmons, L. (2020). Can video support improve attainment? Evaluating the impact of teaching videos on student performance. *ETH Learning and Teaching Journal*, *2*(2), 181–186.

Gibbs, G. (1988). *Learning by doing: A guide to teaching and learning methods*. Oxford: Oxford Centre for Staff and Learning Development, Oxford Brookes University.

Handley, K., & Williams, L. (2011). From copying to learning: Using exemplars to engage students with assessment criteria and feedback. *Assessment & Evaluation in Higher Education*, *36*(1), 95–108. https://doi.org/10.1080/02602930903201669

Jones, S. H. (1996). Crits—An Examination. *Journal of Art & Design Education*, *15*(2), 133–141. https://doi.org/https://doi.org/10.1111/j.1476-8070.1996.tb00660.x

Kirby, N. F., & Downs, C. T. (2007). Self-assessment and the disadvantaged student: Potential for encouraging self-regulated learning? *Assessment & Evaluation in Higher Education*, *32*(4), 475–494. https://doi.org/10.1080/02602930600896464

Langan, A. M., Shuker, D. M., Cullen, W. R., Penney, D., Preziosi, R. F., & Wheater, C. P. (2008). Relationships between student characteristics and self-, peer and tutor evaluations of oral presentations. *Assessment & Evaluation in Higher Education*, *33*(2), 179–190. www.informaworld.com/10.1080/02602930701292498

Micari, M., & Calkins, S. (2019). Is it OK to ask? The impact of instructor openness to questions on student help-seeking and academic outcomes. *Active Learning in Higher Education*, *22*(2), 143–157. https://doi.org/10.1177/1469787419846620

Panadero, E., Andrade, H., & Brookhart, S. (2018). Fusing self-regulated learning and formative assessment: A roadmap of where we are, how we got here, and where we are going. *The Australian Educational Researcher*, *45*(1), 13–31. https://doi.org/10.1007/ s13384-018-0258-y

Race, P. (2019). *The lecturer's toolkit: A practical guide to assessment, learning and teaching* (5th ed.). Abingdon: Routledge.

Rolfe, G. (2002). Reflective practice: Where now? *Nurse Education in Practice*, *2*(1), 21–29.

Sridharan, B., & Boud, D. (2019). The effects of peer judgements on teamwork and self-assessment ability in collaborative group work. *Assessment & Evaluation in Higher Education*, 1–16. https://doi.org/10.1080/02602938.2018.1545898

To, J., Panadero, E., & Carless, D. (2021). A systematic review of the educational uses and effects of exemplars. *Assessment & Evaluation in Higher Education*, 1–16. https://doi.org/10.1080/02602938.2021.2011134

8

MARKING AND FEEDBACK

Chapter overview

This chapter explores:

- The processes of marking and feedback
- Making judgements
- Constructing useful feedback efficiently
- Moderating samples of submissions and feedback

Introduction

Finally, we arrive at the chapter that covers the assessment work which may feel most exposing to teachers: the processes of making and explaining judgements on students' work, and of providing constructive feedback to inform future work. I use the word 'exposing' because this work is scrutinised more systematically than the other important aspects of assessment that we have covered in preceding chapters. Students obviously care greatly about their grades, and hopefully about their feedback too. Your colleagues care about whether students can move from your module to theirs with appropriate knowledge and competence. University managers and leaders care about the progress of students and the reputation of the institution, which may be affected by a perception of inappropriate standards of achievement, either high or low. Professional bodies and regulators care about whether students are appropriately prepared for safe practice in the workplace. National quality regulators care about whether standards are being maintained. With all of these stakeholders having an interest in what you are doing, you need to feel confident in your ability to make good judgements about student submissions in the time available to you.

If your assignment has been carefully designed, planned, and supported in the ways suggested in Chapters 5 and 6, then marking and feedback should be straightforward, or at least as straightforward as making judgements on complex pieces of student work could ever be. You will have been thinking about your expectations of the student work throughout the course, and, through formative work, will have an idea of where students are relative to the assignment task and its marking criteria or scheme. Through the same processes, students should also feel prepared and confident in their own ability to demonstrate their achievements through the task.

Of course, this book is intended to support you through a range of situations other than this hopeful scenario. Maybe you are new to teaching in higher education and don't know where to start. Maybe you have been given marking to do in a subject area you are familiar with, but not expert in. Maybe you didn't design the assignment yourself, and don't share or didn't understand the original creator's vision of its purpose and structure. Maybe your first attempt at the marking criteria weren't quite aligned to your expectations of the task, or of students working at this level. Maybe you couldn't follow through on all of your planning, or something happened during the module which affected everyone's ability to engage with the course content (tutor absence, missing resources, global pandemic, maybe).

All of these situations are plausible when you are a member of a teaching team in a university, and you should have confidence in your ability to carry out the task. To have been appointed to the role of a university teacher, you must have extensive subject knowledge and should be able to make judgements on undergraduate and taught postgraduate courses on a range of topics, even if they aren't all in your own specialist area. In this chapter, we will take a structured approach to marking and feedback that should help you to approach these tasks with confidence and maybe even enjoyment.

Marking and feedback are usually carried out together, but they have different purposes, and we will explore them as separate but linked processes.

Planning marking and feedback

This is going to seem like an obvious statement, but you do need to plan ahead when it comes to the management of submissions. You know when they are coming in, and you need to put aside time for this work, and all professionals will clearly be able to schedule this. However, this advice is included to encourage discussion in a teaching team about how to approach marking, feedback, and moderation so that they are carried out to expected standards and in agreed timeframes. Even if you are the only person marking the work, you will find it useful to put the marking into your diary so that you can protect the time needed to do it properly.

Digital and physical submissions

When you are planning the marking of physical or digital items which are submitted, such as essays, artworks, examination scripts, or reports, you will be managing a process where marking is carried out in the marker's own time, so you only need to organise the scheduling in a general way in the first instance. Some of the questions you will find useful are:

- What is the submission date?
- What is the date when marks are required?
- Should moderation be completed before this date?
- How many teachers are involved in the marking?
- How many submissions should each teacher mark?
- As an estimate, how long do you expect marking each submission to take?
- How many submissions can be marked per day, taking into account the need for breaks and other work being done at the same time?
- Are there likely to be late submissions (due to mitigating circumstances, or accommodations for disabilities)? If so, how many, and what is the last date they will arrive?

The answers to these questions should help you to put together a plan that looks something like Table 8.1. As an individual marker, you can then block out time in your diary for each day during this period when you need to be marking, spreading out the work. Try to stick to this plan: trying to mark too many submissions per day will tire you out and may be unfair to students; leaving the assignments to the last minute will be very stressful.

If you are responsible for allocating submissions to markers, think about the distribution so that it is as random as possible – for instance, every fifth student by student number (for five markers). Note that moderation could start once there is a large enough sample of work, and before the last submissions have been marked. If your assessment design is as robust as it should be, there is no need to allocate submissions according to the tutor or supervisor who has had most contact with the student; it should be possible for someone else to mark the student's work and decide on the same grade and comments.

Table 8.1 Example planner for a physical or digital submission. Note that this planner assumes a four-week turnround from submission to return of marks and feedback

Key dates	Week beginning				
	01 October	08 January	15 January	22 January	29 January
Plan sent to all markers with provisional allocation of submissions	▓				
Main submission date		▓			
Last submission date (special circumstances)				▓	
Final allocation of submissions to markers (if needed)		▓			
Marking period: need detailed plan for each individual		▓	▓		
Moderation period: send sample of submissions and marks to moderators during this period				▓	▓
Marks to university administration					▓
Return date to students					▓

Events

If the assignment is based on an activity which must take place at a certain time, such as a performance, a presentation, or an event, then you will need to plan more specific times and dates. The same kinds of questions apply to the planning, but the process of marking will be slightly different. Because the event is transient, and can't easily be viewed by a moderator, marking would usually be carried out in pairs. If this isn't possible, then a moderator might sample a few different events on the day of assessment, or you could video a sample.

You also need to plan how you will finalise the marking and feedback. It's a good idea to complete this soon after the events, because it can be difficult to remember details without the artefact to refer to, which you would have if moderating an essay. You can keep video or other evidence from the event, such as a PowerPoint file or reflective summary from the students, but you will find it easier to complete the task quickly. If you are working in a pair, you might decide to do this on the same day as the event; if there are multiple pairs, you might want to have a discussion together after all events have been completed.

Table 8.2 Example planner for an event-based assessment

Key dates	Week beginning				
	01 October	08 January	15 January	22 January	29 January
Plan sent to all markers with dates for marking events	▓				
Main event date(s)		▓			
Event dates for special circumstances				▓	▓
Finalisation of grades and feedback		▓	▓	▓	
Moderation period				▓	▓
Marks to university administration					▓
Return date to students					▓

Marking

Time management

So, you've got your marking schedule in front of you, and access to all the submissions allocated to you. You've tidied the house, put the laundry on, and checked that the cat doesn't need to go out (if you have one – if you don't, you may have spent some time considering whether a cat is a good idea). There is no choice but to get on with the task. I'm only partly joking; procrastination is known to be linked to the task of marking (Ang, 2012; Casto, 2017, but only look this one up if you are already procrastinating) and you will probably have many anecdotes about things you and colleagues might do to avoid getting on with it. Thinking back to Chapter 5, there is hope that designing your own assignment task may transform your attitude to the responsibility of marking, seeing it instead as something to look forward to as your students demonstrate their achievements at the end of a period of working with you (Durfee, 1993). But, in reality, it may take a while to settle to the task. It's only partly procrastination. It's worth remembering that the responsibility of marking may also weigh quite heavily, and make it difficult to get started.

If you are marking an event-based assignment, the timescale is fixed for you. There is no alternative but to get on with it. You can apply the same principle to submissions that are physical or digital, that you are marking to your own schedule. Make a plan for the marking session, with the names and times you will grade each piece of student work, and just get on with it. You can award yourself breaks and treats as part of the schedule (whatever works for you: a coffee, five minutes on Twitter or other social media of your choice, dealing with five emails, a walk round the block). Once you've settled into the rhythm, you should start enjoying seeing what students have done and begin to feel confident in your judgements.

Making judgements

We can't put it off any longer. Marking involves making judgements. We've already discussed the complexity of this and the difficulties in being accurate and equitable. First, review the rubric or marking scheme so that you refamiliarise yourself with the key criteria. With a rubric for holistic marking, you need to read through (or watch) the whole submission before starting to make a judgement. Then look at your criteria, and judge where the piece of work sits in each part of your rubric. In many cases, these decisions will be relatively straightforward, and the pattern of judgements for each criterion will let you decide a mark quite easily and reproducibly, in that the same pattern would lead to the same grade each time.

Sometimes, the structure of the submission will have led you to focus on one criterion, without thinking about the others as you read through or watched the submission. So you may need to repeat the process, consciously thinking about the criteria you didn't focus on previously. Perhaps you just need to skim one of the sections to make your mind up, perhaps you need to read or watch the whole piece with the same level of attention. There will be variation in the time you need to judge each submission, because of the complexity of each individual piece.

With an analytical marking scheme, you are making a series of individual judgements about elements of the submission, using your rubric as you work through each stage of the piece of work.

The work of converting judgements to grades is made when your rubrics are created, so your final overall grade for the piece of work will be determined from the grades you allocated to each box in the rubric and applying any weighting you chose for each row.

Take regular breaks and be prepared to return to something you graded at the beginning of the day to see if you still feel the same way about it. If the criteria are valid, reliable, and equitable, this will be the case, but checking is a valuable self-moderation activity.

Academic integrity

Whatever the purposes of the individual assignment, submissions of student work are intended to be their own work, with the contributions of others clearly acknowledged. All universities will penalise students who do not submit their own work; some countries may have national guidance on this, or it may be left to the discretion of the institution.

We considered ways to reduce cheating in Chapter 5, but you do need to consider the possibility of dishonesty when you are marking a piece of student work, particularly when you didn't have the opportunity to design the assignment task yourself. Before you start marking, make sure that you are familiar with your responsibilities in relation to your own university's regulations about what is considered to be cheating and the evidence that may be needed to prove it.

Detection of academic dishonesty can be challenging. Occasionally you might notice chunks of text or computer code or diagrams that are identical to another piece of work you have marked, or to your own notes, or to a piece of work you are familiar with. If written work is plagiarised, the dishonesty may be picked up through clues such as changes in text or presentation style (such as a change in fonts indicating pasting from another document), or the use of a different form of your language (e.g. American English when you are marking in the UK). However, students who are determined to cheat are likely to be careful about correcting such inconsistencies, and these signs are less useful than they might have been in the past. You might wonder about the inclusion of material not covered in your course, or references not available in your own library, but on the other hand, you might have wanted students to develop their sources outside the basics you provide. Work which seems very different from formative submissions may also ring alarm bells, but if you have very large groups and don't have the opportunity to get to know students and their work well, or are marking anonymously, then you are unlikely to notice.

Many universities subscribe to software which compares student submissions to other published work, and using such applications may be routine, or automatic, at your institution. These systems provide you with a report on the similarity of the student assignment to other materials in the database. In itself, this doesn't create a case for dishonesty. Sometimes a high level of similarity is due to poor use of quotations and referencing, using too many quotations rather than developing their own ideas, and/or failing to identify them as such clearly. These factors should be accounted for in your marking criteria, leading to a lower grade.

Another form of academic dishonesty, contract cheating, is very difficult to detect with certainty. The quality of purchased work is very variable (Sutherland-Smith & Dullaghan, 2019) so you may not be able to tell easily, and if you are using anonymous marking, you can't compare what you get with your knowledge of the student. One study which asked experienced markers to grade a mixture of purchased and genuine student work found that the markers identified bought work 62% of the time (Dawson & Sutherland-Smith, 2017). You can look out for some of the signs mentioned in the previous paragraph on plagiarism, of course, but the limitations are the same.

If you suspect that a submission may not be the student's own work, you will need to follow your university's regulations for reporting this. Deciding whether to sanction students for academic dishonesty is a quasi-legal process which would usually be subject to an appeal, if a penalty is applied. There may be a specified process for collecting evidence, but if one doesn't exist, the following basic steps should be used:

1   Make notes about your suspicions, including examples of the alleged dishonesty.
2   Distinguish between poor academic practice, such as not making quotations clear and missed or misplaced citations, and the integration of other people's work as their own without acknowledgement.
3   Write a short report summarising your suspicions and appending the evidence.
4   Share the report with a peer, to check it seems credible. Sometimes this person will be identified in your university's regulations (for instance, a head of department or nominated academic integrity co-ordinator).

In Chapter 5, we mentioned the possibility of designing in the option of an oral examination to question a student about their submission, if you suspect that it is not all their own work. The ability to respond to questions about the assignment under examination conditions should satisfy you that the student has achieved the learning outcomes, although it wouldn't rule out dishonesty in the assignment. It could help you to decide whether to proceed with an investigation and report, though.

If you are sure, on the balance of probability, that the student has cheated, the next steps will depend on your university regulations. It would be usual for the student to be invited to a meeting where this evidence will be presented and they have a chance to respond. You may or may not be included in such a meeting, to explain your suspicions. Students should always be invited to bring a representative with them to such a meeting, which can be very stressful. In my experience, most students who have cheated will admit to it at this stage, so that further investigation and formal hearings are unnecessary. To reflect this, university penalties will usually have a scale of severity: a first offence might be treated as a developmental event, with the submission being failed, but giving an opportunity to resubmit for a reduced grade. A second or third offence could result in a complete failure for that module or removal from the course.

These kinds of meetings often also result in the student declaring mitigating circumstances to excuse their behaviour. Students should of course declare in advance if they will have difficulties in completing an assignment, and there will be systems for doing so. But students may find it hard to admit, or not even understand, that they won't get the task finished on time, or feel that they will be labelled as failures for asking for extra time, and so don't use these systems. They are then confronted with what they may see as the limited options of cheating, and chancing detection, or not submitting their assignments and definitely getting a zero mark. Such excuses may not be accommodated in your university's regulations: dishonesty is dishonesty.

However, here again we come up against the issue of assessment processes doing double duty. The university has to be fair to all students by making it clear that cheating is wrong and will be penalised, but it also has a duty of care to the student who declares their problems, even if that happens after cheating, which is an attempt to gain an unfair advantage, has taken place. A developmental scale of penalties can help to mitigate this tension by penalising the cheating student, but allowing them to get back on track in the future.

You will see that identifying and proving academic dishonesty is complex and time-consuming, but it is essential that you engage fully with the process. If a student can gain an unfair advantage in your assignment, then academic standards are not being upheld, the student is not learning what they should, and other students who behave honestly are penalised. You can reduce the likelihood of cheating by using some of the suggestions in Chapter 5. If you aren't yet designing your own tasks, bring these ideas up in discussion with colleagues.

Feedback

Revisiting the purpose of feedback

In Chapter 6, we looked at the design of a feedback strategy as part of the overall planning of an assignment task, and gave a brief introduction to what is now a very extensive literature on feedback, which includes several models of good practice.

Producing feedback

Reviews of feedback studies show that there is no magical ideal structure for feedback, as teachers, students, relationships, and subject contexts vary so much. The models we have discussed above are just intended to help you to structure it. Whatever approach you use to communicate feedback on summative assessment, focus on the purpose of your feedback when thinking about what to say or write. Your feedback, like all other aspects of your teaching, should be designed to support student action in the future. It should also be manageable to produce, and enable students to make improvements.

It is a persistent myth that negative feedback needs to be balanced with positive feedback: the so-called feedback sandwich, in which the negative message represents the filling, flanked by two pieces of positive feedback. Molloy et al. (2020) point out that this notion of positive/negative feedback provided by the teacher reinforces the idea that feedback is something that teachers do and students receive. Hyland and Hyland (2001) found that the mix of positive and negative feedback could also be quite confusing to students.

As we have seen, students' ability to act on feedback is complex and dependent on their understanding of its purposes and the provision of clear routes to act on it. The small number of studies that have investigated the feedback sandwich approach, which have mostly been in the context of medical education or in workplace feedback, have generally found that these factors are much more important than the particular structure (Beaulieu et al., 2019; Parkes et al., 2013). Note that a study which compared sandwich feedback with corrective feedback (which described mistakes and showed model solutions), or no feedback at all, showed that the sandwich feedback led to students spending more time on their next tasks (Prochazka et al., 2020), but it was a fairly limited study using computer-marked assessments, and with only ten minutes between first and second tests.

With all of this in mind, here are some tips for producing actionable feedback:

1   Focus on a small number of actions students can take: keep the feedback brief. Students will not be able to process a great deal of detail.

2   Do say if an aspect of the submission was very effective, or if it added nothing to the work, and explain why, in measured tones. If praise or criticism is very strong in tone, students are likely to focus on these statements rather than the proposed actions.

Example: Don't say: The inclusion of Smith's work was excellent, well done.
Do say: The inclusion of Smith's work was something I wasn't expecting at this level of study, and you linked it effectively to your argument about classroom behaviour.

3   Don't use hedging language: it can be misinterpreted. If you have advice, make it clear.

Example: Don't say: It might be a good idea to spend more time on the primary sources in your next assignment.
Do say: In your next assignment, spend more time thinking about how the primary sources link to your research question and how you can use them to support your analysis.

4   Only comment on those aspects of the assignment which were relevant to the assessment. For instance, you may realise that students have put in a lot of effort, but this isn't being assessed, and won't be reflected in the grades, so it isn't helpful to acknowledge it here.

Example: Don't say: I can see that you have tried hard, but you haven't addressed all of the learning outcomes.
Do say: In your next assignment, put aside time to understand what is being asked in the assignment brief, and ask your teacher for help if you don't fully understand it. That way, you will make the best use of your time.

5   Do use language which links back to the assignment task and which is consistent with the grade the student received. In suggesting actions, you can use phrases from the marking rubric for a higher band.

Example: You made sensible recommendations for the customer based on a limited analysis of their situation. In your next assignment, consider whether you can offer a wider range of possibilities, taking into account their future needs as well as their current ones.

These strategies can be difficult to employ; we are all accustomed to academic writing, which is full of hedging statements, and you have read plenty in this book. Hyland and Hyland (2001, p. 199) suggest that teachers wish to be kind and to develop good relationships with students, which may lead to the use of 'mitigation devices' to soften the impact of their comments. They point out that this can lead to confusion, and later research on feedback has shown that it is important to be direct, so that students understand your advice (Dawson et al., 2018; Henderson et al., 2021).

You will find that you develop a series of stock phrases or statements that you use, and it may be useful to collect these into a file, or to use a digital marking tool to help with adding them to a feedback report.

Moderation

If you are reviewing a sample of student work and teacher grades and feedback as an internal moderator or external examiner, then you will need to switch your focus from individual submissions to the review of standards and processes. As a moderator, you are giving feedback to your peers, and not to students directly. For individual assignments, you will probably be asked to comment on aspects of the assessment process, compared to your knowledge and experience of similar assignments, in relation to questions such as:

- Do you agree that the submissions are ranked appropriately?
- Do you agree that the submissions you reviewed were in the correct grade bands?
- Were the grades awarded clearly related to the rubric?
- Was the quality and detail of feedback appropriate?
- Did the feedback identify areas for development?
- Did the feedback comment positively on areas that the student had done well?
- Did the feedback relate to the marking criteria?

If you are looking at a range of assignment tasks, you may also be asked to compare standards and approaches across modules.

Conclusion

Assessment is a big responsibility but working through the process systematically should make it more manageable for you, and allow you to focus on the positive aspects: seeing what students have achieved and providing them with feedback to improve in the future. Students will remember the care you have put into your assessment process.

Further reading

There is practical guidance on marking in Biggs and Tang (2011). Further ideas on sustainable feedback can be found in Boud and Falchikov (2007) and Boud and Molloy (2012).

References

Ang, N. (2012). Procrastination as rational weakness of will. *The Journal of Value Inquiry*, *46*(4), 403–416.

Beaulieu, A. M., Kim, B. S., Topor, D. R., & Dickey, C. C. (2019). Seeing is believing: An exploration of what residents value when they receive feedback. *Academic Psychiatry*, *43*(5), 507–511. https://doi.org/10.1007/s40596-019-01071-5

Biggs, J., & Tang, C. (2011). *Teaching for quality learning at university* (4th ed.). Maidenhead: Open University Press/McGraw Hill.

Boud, D., & Falchikov, N. (Eds.). (2007). *Rethinking assessment in higher education: Learning for the longer term*. Abingdon: Routledge.

Boud, D., & Molloy, E. (2012). Rethinking models of feedback for learning: The challenge of design. *Assessment & Evaluation in Higher Education*, *38*(6), 698–712. https://doi.org/10.1080/02602938.2012.691462

Casto, W. R. (2017). The abiding importance of procrastination in grading law-school final examinations. Corpus ID: 80609927.

Dawson, P., Henderson, M., Mahoney, P., Phillips, M., Ryan, T., Boud, D., & Molloy, E. (2018). What makes for effective feedback: Staff and student perspectives. *Assessment & Evaluation in Higher Education*, 1–12. https://doi.org/10.1080/02602938.2018.1467877

Dawson, P., & Sutherland-Smith, W. (2017). Can markers detect contract cheating? Results from a pilot study. *Assessment & Evaluation in Higher Education*, 1–8. https://doi.org/10.1080/02602938.2017.1336746

Durfee, M. (1993). The quick fix: Grading exams as the payoff. *College Teaching*, *41*(1), 25–25. https://doi.org/10.1080/87567555.1993.9926779

Henderson, M., Ryan, T., Boud, D., Dawson, P., Phillips, M., Molloy, E., & Mahoney, P. (2021). The usefulness of feedback. *Active Learning in Higher Education*, *22*(3), 229–243. https://doi.org/10.1177/1469787419872393

Hyland, F., & Hyland, K. (2001). Sugaring the pill: Praise and criticism in written feedback. *Journal of Second Language Writing*, *10*(3), 185–212. https://doi.org/https://doi.org/10.1016/S1060-3743(01)00038-8

Molloy, E., Ajjawi, R., Bearman, M., Noble, C., Rudland, J., & Ryan, A. (2020). Challenging feedback myths: Values, learner involvement and promoting effects beyond the immediate task. *Medical Education*, *54*(1), 33–39. https://doi.org/https://doi.org/10.1111/medu.13802

Parkes, J., Abercrombie, S., & McCarty, T. (2013). Feedback sandwiches affect perceptions but not performance. *Advances in Health Sciences Education*, *18*(3), 397–407.

Prochazka, J., Ovcari, M., & Durinik, M. (2020). Sandwich feedback: The empirical evidence of its effectiveness. *Learning and Motivation*, *71*, 101649. https://doi.org/https://doi.org/10.1016/j.lmot.2020.101649

Sutherland-Smith, W., & Dullaghan, K. (2019). You don't always get what you pay for: User experiences of engaging with contract cheating sites. *Assessment & Evaluation in Higher Education*, 1–15. https://doi.org/10.1080/02602938.2019.1576028

9

ASSESSING WITH CONFIDENCE

Chapter overview

This chapter explores:

- Using data to review the effectiveness of assessment and feedback
- Inclusive and sustainable assessment
- Developing as a confident assessor in higher education

Introduction

We began the book by questioning many of the familiar building blocks of assessment design, such as tradition, expectations, and previous experiences, before creating new foundations based on academic judgement and a systematic approach to each aspect of the assessment lifecycle. The idea was to give you confidence in your own decision-making so that you feel in control of all parts of assessment and of your own ability to design, support, and manage assessments which work best for you, your students, and your subject area.

There is no perfect way to assess anything in higher education. This book is intended to give you confidence in making decisions about assessment that are right for you, your academic discipline, your institution and, most importantly, your students. A confident assessor will reflect and review regularly on the way things have gone with a task, taking into account the views of all stakeholders.

The last part of the assessment lifecycle is to review the assignment task and to identify any changes you might need to make, both for the individual task and for your own professional development. In this chapter we will consider the data that you might collect and use to complete this process, and how to interpret findings so that you can keep on developing.

Reflection and review

The best time to carry out a thorough review of an assignment task is immediately after a marking period, towards the end of the assessment lifecycle. Depending on your responsibilities in assessment, you may have access to a range of different quantitative and qualitative data which will help you to review aspects of the assignment task and consider changes, as well as to identify areas for your own development in the future. What follows is a selection of questions you can ask about the task. You may not have answers to all of these, and you will probably think of additional ones which are relevant to your own practice.

How many students passed?

This is the most basic measure of the success of the assignment. If students put in the minimum work expected during the module, then they should be expected to pass. If more students than you expect have failed, you can think about whether the task detail or marking criteria need adjustment, or whether something in the teaching and preparation for the assignment should be changed. In the short term, you should discuss with the person who has moderated the work whether the grades are a fair reflection of the students' achievements, as an additional check on standards, ideally before grades are released to students.

How many students got the highest possible grades?

If you have a range of grades available, rather than a simple pass/fail system, was it possible for some students to get the maximum marks available? Did you feel that the work they produced was really exceptional? If more students than you expected did exceptionally well, you should discuss with the person who has moderated the work whether the grades are a fair reflection of the students' achievements, as an additional check on standards, ideally before grades are released to students.

Were the students' marks comparable with their other modules?

This isn't any kind of absolute measure of assignment success. Students may be taking a wide variety of modules with different types of assessment, and it could be difficult to make meaningful comparisons. However, you would expect students at the same level of study on the same course to be achieving roughly similar grades in different modules. If not, you would have to question the validity and reliability of the different tasks. This is an important conversation to have with all teachers responsible for assessment across the same level of study in a course. Reviewing each other's assignment briefs and moderating each other's marking and feedback will help with understanding intention and outcomes, and with discussions about consistency. It isn't enough to say that a particular assignment was a statistical analysis and students find that difficult, or that these students all prefer to design an artefact and so do better on such a task. Task design needs to take into account the intended learning outcomes, but also how students can demonstrate achievement appropriately. You need to identify the purpose of choosing a task which students find more difficult, or one which they prefer. As ever, there is not a simple solution. Perhaps the professional body requires a particular type of statistical analysis, in which case you might want to open discussions within the discipline nationally about the best way to support students to perform well in such a task. Student preference is not a bad thing, but if you think it is artificially inflating grades on a task, you might want to look at the marking rubric to ensure that your expectations for performance are met.

Did you find it easy to assign work to different grade bands?

If the marking criteria are clear, with well-differentiated grade bands, then the choice of grade from the marking rubric should be quite straightforward. If this isn't the case, think about whether the wording is correct. Are the adjectives you have used to distinguish different grades clear enough? Are you asking for the right evidence against each learning outcome? As we discussed in Chapter 6, it is difficult to get this right first time, and the best time to review a rubric is just after you have used it – don't wait until the beginning of the next teaching session, as you may have forgotten what you found difficult to use by then.

Were you happy with the range of grades achieved generally?

Were you able to discriminate between different submissions, so that students' achievements were reflected in the range of grades you awarded? If not, you could look at the wording of the marking criteria to differentiate the grade bands more strongly.

Did you enjoy seeing the students' work?

You and the students have worked together across the module or course, leading up to the submissions, and it should be possible for you to enjoy seeing what they have achieved. If you find you are looking at many similar submissions, or finding them rather boring, think about what you would rather have seen instead. Would a change to the assignment description, or to the marking criteria, allow for some creativity in student thinking? Can you reward the consideration of an alternative approach?

If you have a lot of marking, it can be difficult to see beyond the pressure of getting it finished, and making the work more interesting might be difficult, but can you adapt the marking process next time to share the work with colleagues, and reciprocate by marking something they teach? This can be a way to make things more interesting for all of you, as well as helping to build your collective understanding of what is taught and assessed on the course and contributing to the social construction of standards.

Were there any common misconceptions or errors made by students across all of the submissions?

Ideally, students will have been working on their assignment submissions right through the module, and will have asked the right questions during the module, so that they were well prepared for their final work, but it can happen that there are some common challenges which you will only see when you are marking the submissions. Don't feel bad about it if it happens. You may need to take them into account when making your final judgements about the work, ideally before the grades are returned to students. In your review, think about what you can do to adjust the assignment brief, the teaching, or the marking rubric in order to reduce the chances of it happening again.

Was there any evidence, or suspicion, of academic dishonesty?

We considered ways of identifying academic dishonesty in Chapter 8. Clear cases of misconduct should of course be managed according to your institutional regulations. Very often, these will be individual situations which are not an artefact of the assessment design, but it is always worth considering if there is anything in the assignment brief which could be adapted to make it more difficult for this to happen. See Chapter 5 for some ideas on this.

It is also possible that you suspect dishonesty but can't prove it according to university rules. You will have to give individual students the benefit of the doubt, but again you can think about what has given rise to your suspicion, and whether you can do something to make this less likely in the future.

Were grades distributed equitably and independently of individual characteristics such as disability, ethnic origin, or gender?

These particular data are often better considered at departmental or institutional level, rather than for individual modules. It can be quite difficult to look at them on a small scale; you may not have access to all of the data, or your cohort size may be too small for you to identify any variations. However, even a crude analysis can be helpful in giving you a sense of how things are going and whether you need to pay attention to anything in particular.

Are there other ways you can enable your students to demonstrate their achievements which better suit their previous experiences? Are they able to demonstrate what they have brought with them to the study of your module and completion of the task you designed? If you have made adjustments to the task to support students with a particular disability, can these be offered more widely, to provide choice for all students? If you don't want to do this, is it because you think it would make the assignment easier for other students? In that case, maybe the adjustments are providing an unexpected advantage, and should themselves be reviewed. Go back to the design decisions in Chapter 5 if you want some further ideas on choice, or look at the options suggested in Part 3 for the type of task you are using.

Was technology used effectively to support you and your students?

Some of the technology used to manage assessment may be under your control, such as the choice of format for the submission, while other aspects may be determined by the university or department, such as the use of a virtual learning environment or assignment submission tool. Think carefully about the process of managing the assessment, such as distributing assignment briefs, answering questions about the task, finding and grading the submissions, managing the moderation, or returning the feedback to students? Did you find any part of the process frustrating? Were you using digital tools for any parts of the process? Could you make improvements to the process, or ask for some help with doing so? You don't need to have an understanding of everything that may be available, but the clearer you can be about what you would like to happen, the more chance there is that a technology specialist will be able to suggest some adaptations to settings, or different tools, to help.

What do the moderation reports say?

Think of internal and external moderation as a kind of peer observation. The moderator is verifying academic standards and process, and is also in a position to give you feedback on your assessment practice. The most important information to act on is in relation to expected standards: did your students demonstrate their achievements to standards which are comparable in other modules and in other institutions teaching the same subject? If not, you will need to make some quick decisions about the grades, ideally before grades are released to students.

To support development of the task, you can also encourage moderators to make suggestions about how the task might be adapted, whether the marking rubric is clear, and whether you are supporting students in the way you give feedback. Such comments should help you to think about what you could change to make the assignment even better, but remember that your colleagues may not all have become as skilled at feedback as you – never take comments personally. They are about the task and its design, not you as a person and teacher.

What do the students say?

The nature of modern modularised higher education is that student evaluations are often collected before they have had their assignments marked, and often ask mainly about the teaching, rather than the assignment itself. This may mean that you need to make additional effort to find out what they think about the assignment.

You can try asking them for comments about the assignment to be submitted along-side the task, but they may feel that the comments would affect the marking. The evaluation can be carried out just after the assignment, but this can be a time when students are feeling quite emotional about the work they have put in and their potential grades, and so are not always as objective as they might be later on. You may not see those students again during their course, so it can be difficult to get their feedback after you have returned the grades, but this may be the best time to find out whether they enjoyed the assignment, whether they felt confident preparing the submissions, whether they understood their grade and feedback, and if anything would have helped them to demonstrate their achievements more easily. As with peer review, remember not to take student feedback to heart: it is to be used to improve the assignment for future students. Assessment can have a strong emotional impact, which may affect the language used in evaluation – take that into account.

Other stakeholders

As we have previously discussed, a lot of people have views on assessment. The frequency with which you solicit the opinions of external stakeholders, such as professional bodies and employer representatives, will depend on the context. If they are directly involved in assessment, such as an employer helping to assess a presentation or creating a live project brief, then you can ask informally for their views at the time, or by email afterwards. If they have indirect involvement, it may be difficult to get detailed feedback about individual tasks, because they won't be so familiar with them, but you can ask general questions about their expectations of student achievements, to make sure that you keep up to date with changes. Many employer groups, such as chambers of commerce or industry bodies, carry out regular surveys of their members in relation to graduate recruitment and expectations, so it is always worth seeing what these show and cross-checking your assignments against these.

You also need to consider how well your assignment task(s) contribute to the overall course aims. It may be an amazing standalone activity, but does it fit in with what everyone else is doing? Is it clear how this assignment moves the student along in terms of the final qualification outcomes?

Within your department or the university as a whole, there may be an assessment community of practice in which colleagues discuss assessment generally and may be willing to do a peer review of your tasks from a detached perspective. This can be very useful for seeing how your tasks look to someone new before you test them out with students.

You might not ask everyone involved in assessment in the university how things are going after each assignment, but it is worth thinking about what information you can get from other people we have talked about less so far. Colleagues responsible for administering and supporting parts of the assessment process may well have views about how well certain tasks fit into other university systems. While processes shouldn't determine academic decisions, an open discussion about practicality and timings can be helpful to make sure that you are getting the best from any support systems. Are you involving the library team at the right stage? Do the technical team have any ideas to improve management of practical work? Can your students get more help with their writing skills early in the assignment? Are there special invigilation arrangements which you aren't aware of? Can the technology team help you to find a better tool to support marking and feedback?

You can also give feedback on how things work for you. Are quality processes onerous? Do you have any suggestions for making reporting more streamlined? Is there more data that would help you to improve the assignments?

Conclusion

A confident assessor understands that they can only do their best, and that assessment is a process of continuous development. You take the decisions that you think are best for a particular time and context, and then you reflect on the outcomes and decide on improvements. The coronavirus pandemic of 2020–22 showed many assessors in higher education that changes to assessment can happen quickly, even if sometimes enforced changes are not the ones we might have picked if we had had the time to reflect properly. Some students have found that the changes have made assessment more accessible to them;

others will have been made anxious and bewildered by them. Some teachers will have found that simply switching to an online form of the same assignment task has been problematic in terms of standards and academic honesty; others will have rejoiced in the creative thinking students have done in response to a change in submission method.

Many people will be asking themselves if they have to return to pre-pandemic approaches to assessment, or if long-term changes are possible. The book contains many ideas for adapting and updating assessment at all stages in the lifecycle. Some of those ideas will be terrible in your context, while others may be just what you were looking for. You will also have many brilliant ideas which aren't covered here, which I haven't read or thought about. Confident assessment requires elements of choice for both teachers and their students, and making informed choices needs sound knowledge and understanding. You don't need to launch into huge changes immediately: build up your decision-making skills and confidence by making small choices in the parts of the assessment lifecycle you have control over, then work up to having further conversations and generating ideas with colleagues and students. The more we discuss, analyse, and improve all aspects of assessment, the more we will collectively improve our own assessment literacy and that of the sector.

Further reading

This article on managing our responses to feedback is very useful in helping to think constructively about our own practices (Arthur, 2009).

Reference

Arthur, L. (2009). From performativity to professionalism: Lecturers' responses to student feedback. *Teaching in Higher Education*, *14*(4), 441–454. www.informaworld.com/10.1080/13562510903050228

PART 3

CHOOSING ASSIGNMENT TASKS AND FEEDBACK TOOLS

This part of the book provides practical summaries of a range of assignment tasks and feedback approaches, highlighting their features in relation to the considerations outlined in Parts 1 and 2. These are representative examples to give you some ideas about your own assessment design, not a definitive reference: you will make your own choices and create new tasks to suit your own context. Refer back to Chapters 5 and 6 for a detailed discussion of the decisions you need to make about each aspect of assignment design.

You will be able to find case studies of the use of the tasks and feedback approaches in your own general subject areas by searching an online catalogue of higher education journals, and you will find this useful to identify details and particular considerations in your discipline. I have not included a list of such studies here, as there are so many.

10
ASSIGNMENT TASKS

The assignment tasks are grouped into two parts: coursework, tasks which are completed over a period of time, and examinations, which are time-constrained. For each task, you will find some guidance on a range of aspects of the design:

Description

A short summary of the task.

Level

The level of study at which this is suitable: The numbering system used here is based on the UK *Framework for Higher Education Qualifications* (FHEQ) (QAA, 2008)).

- 3 – Foundation year, pre-University studies

- 4 – First year Bachelor's/ first cycle on the European Credit Transfer System, ECTS

- 5 – Second year Bachelor's / first cycle

- 6 – Final year Bachelor's / first cycle

- 7 – Master's / second cycle

If your national system has four-year Bachelor's degrees, then use level 3 for first year, and level 6 for fourth year. If you are creating modules for taught doctorate level modules, use the Master's level as a reference.

Indicative learning outcomes

What can be assessed with this task? These examples are written in intentionally generic language: every module will have its own detailed context and scope. See Chapter 1 for detailed guidance on writing assessable outcomes.

Key information

What do students need to know and what might you need to consider when you are writing the assignment brief and planning the marking and feedback?

Student choice

Can you give students any agency in this task?

Suitability for groups

A brief indication of whether a task can be used with groups and if so, any additional factors you might consider.

Submission size

You will be working with your own module credit sizes and weightings, so this heading just gives an idea of the minimum size you might need to make a judgement about performance.

Timing

Where should this be situated in a module or programme?

Inclusive practice

Ideas for making the task accessible and inclusive.

Avoiding academic misconduct

How can you design out forms of cheating to gain academic advantage?

Coursework: Not time-constrained

- Article
- Bibliography
- Biography
- Blog
- Case study
- Competence portfolio
- Essay
- Event

- Poster
- Project or dissertation
- Synthesis portfolio or patchwork text

Examination: Time-constrained

- Unseen examination
- Seen examination
- Open-book examination
- Take-home examination
- Objective Structured (Clinical) Examination
- Practical examination
- Multiple-choice test
- Oral examination
- Presentation
- Performance or show

Coursework (non-time-constrained assessment)

Article

Description

Students might be asked to produce an article for an academic journal, or a real or imaginary newsletter, blog, magazine, or newspaper.

Level

This can be set at any level, but the type of article needs to be appropriate: writing something suitable for an academic journal would only be suitable for students at levels 6 or 7. Writing well for other kinds of publication also needs high-level skills, so this would be suitable at these levels too. Novice students (levels 3 and 4) could be asked to write for a newsletter or blog, and you might put less emphasis on the communication skills at these levels.

Indicative learning outcomes

On completion of this task, students will be able to:

- Communicate ideas about [topic] to [defined audience]
- Synthesise complex ideas into a communication suitable for [defined audience]

Key information

The choice of publication could be something related to the subject (e.g. 'an update on latest thinking on XX for *History Today*'), linked to a particular community ('Advice on managing back pain for the *Hulme News*') or company ('What we are doing to gain IiP (Investors in People) status' or 'an explanation of our new strategic aims' for the *Company Newsletter*), or of general interest ('Write a critique of current school health and safety guidance suitable for *The Times*'). The selection of publication will depend on the level of study and the skills to be developed. You could specify the title of the article or ask students to select something appropriate for themselves. If they are selecting a title themselves, then allow time in the assignment planning and add a formative submission for you to check the suitability of the title.

A non-academic article could be accompanied with a short piece which links the article to the work done on the unit, and provides the academic sources used in the article, and/or an appendix which explains how the student went about doing the analysis and summarisation. At level 4, this commentary could be fairly simple and might be worth 20–25% of the total marks for the submission, but you might expect a student at level 6 or 7 to perform a sophisticated reflective analysis of their work, which might be worth up to 50%.

Academic journal style submissions should use the writing style suitable for the discipline. For newspapers, magazines, blogs, and newsletters, the writing should not be academic in style and would not be expected to contain the breadth and depth of analysis of a more traditional academic piece. However, there is a skill to writing well and communicating complex ideas clearly in such a style and some marks should be allocated for this as well as for content. (NB: Blogs as a narrative assignment are discussed separately.)

Student choice

You can offer choice over the title and content of the piece, or the selection of publication. Consider whether this must be a written piece, or whether you could consider a choice of written, audio, video, or drawn submissions. Alternatives may make this more accessible for students with mild to moderate specific learning disabilities. You need to be confident that the submission types are comparable in difficulty and that you can mark them using the same criteria.

Suitability for groups

This could be done in a small group or a pair, as team work on a publication of this kind is very common. Students could complete this work in pairs or small groups. They could each be encouraged to take on different types of task (e.g. background research, interviews, field visit, and photography) to contribute to the final product. The length and degree of polish of the final submission would reflect the number of contributors. If the ability to work in a group is being assessed, then the group could also complete a short submission which explains how roles were allocated and how each contributed to the finished article. They could also peer assess each others' contributions to the task.

Submission size

The length of the piece and the level of language use should reflect the usual house style of a similar publication. That could be 3–5,000 words for an academic article, and perhaps 1,000 words for a blog post or newspaper opinion piece.

Timing

Students need to have a good grasp of the topic before attempting this kind of synthesis, so this needs to be timed for the end of a module.

Inclusive practice

Offering students choice about topic and/or medium is the best way to make this task inclusive. You can allow students to choose a publication which accepts video, audio, or written articles, so that they can work in a medium in which they are comfortable. You could suggest focusing on a comparison with a different country with which they are more familiar, even if you aren't, as long as you feel able to assess their analysis.

Avoiding academic misconduct

Choice is useful here too: make the assignment personal to the individual student. This can be difficult to manage when you have large groups, because you need to check that they have made suitable choices, but it can be done if linked to seminar or tutorial groups, which are smaller.

Bibliography

Description

A bibliography as a separate assessment task usually consists of a set of references with annotations which explain why each source has been selected and how it is relevant to the topic. You can also ask students to explain how they went about finding each source.

Level

It can be used as a key part of the apprenticeship for producing more substantial pieces of academic work. This makes it particularly useful at levels 3–5. It could be used at higher levels as a formative or first assignment in a unit, giving you the opportunity to monitor progress before a piece of writing is submitted at the end of the unit, for instance.

Indicative learning outcomes

On completion of this task, students will be able to:

- Identify appropriate sources for future study on the topic of…
- Use an appropriate search strategy in [the topic area]
- Explain how relevant sources relate to a selected research area
- Work with others to select the most appropriate examples of…

Key information

You should indicate the number of items you want students to find and to write about. You need to be prepared to check the references selected and this is a good reason for setting clear rules about the scope of the bibliography, the kinds of sources which are acceptable for this task (Peer reviewed only? Popular culture? Websites? Newspapers and magazines? Social media? Databases? Primary sources only? Literature reviews? Grey literature?), and the location of such sources (should they be restricted to your own university library, or a certain country? Do you encourage independent searching even if it may lead to inappropriate choices?).

You will find it helpful to consult with your university librarian before confirming the final details of such an assignment and they may be able to offer specific support to students.

Student choice

Students will be finding and choosing their own references, and you may also be able to give them some choice over the topic. You could offer choice over the submission type: perhaps students could be given the option to present their selections verbally, using a video, rather than a written document. If they do this, you would need to ask for a list of references submitted digitally as a file you can check.

Suitability for groups

This could be an individual or group task. The obvious approach for a group would be for students to divide up the work into identification of one or more references each. If the number of references remains the same as you would set for individuals, then a more detailed analysis would be expected, together with an overall commentary on how the work was done in the group and what the overall conclusions are. You could assess the group's reflections on the process of selection and agreement on the final list and what they learned from achieving consensus. This would need to be reflected in the intended learning outcomes – e.g. 'work with others to select the most appropriate examples of…'.

Submission size

This could be a short assignment. You should be able to judge student performance from 5–8 examples, with 100–200 words on each item. Discipline areas will vary, but you could estimate that it might take a student around two or three hours to find an individual high-quality source and write something meaningful about it in relation to the unit content.

Timing

This is a preparatory task and should be set early in a module or programme.

Inclusive practice

In some instances, you may be looking for very specific outcomes from this kind of task, such as identification of particular sources from a canon of literature. In that case, your main aim will be to ensure that everyone gets to a certain point, and inclusive practice should be focused on making sure the right support is in place.

However, if you are focusing on the process of identifying and selecting sources more than a particular product, you could challenge students to:

- Find one source which they think you wouldn't have thought of
- Find one source they think you would disagree with
- Find one source published in a language you don't know but they do (but with a translated synopsis)
- Find one source which is in a different format from a traditional academic paper but which presents ideas in a way that might be used to develop an argument.
- Present a perspective which is at odds with received wisdom in your country or in the discipline

Avoiding academic misconduct

You are asking for a series of short pieces, and these can be easy to copy and for a contract cheating service to produce. In some disciplinary areas, the number of suitable sources may be small, which means students will use the same references. Minimise the possibility of misconduct by

- keeping the titles topical
- focusing on personal interpretations of the sources and their importance
- asking for the inclusion of one or more sources which aren't relevant together with the explanation of why not
- encouraging discussion in class of the process of searching
- making it a group task and setting aside class time for groups to work on their selections, to emphasise process rather than product

Biography

Description

A biography is a description of someone's life, or an aspect of it. It is not just a task for creative writing students or historians; it can be an interesting way to encourage students to find out more about relevant people in the discipline, encouraging them to uncover context and help them to relate what happens in their discipline to other things in the world. By tracing and analysing someone's career path, they can see how study or practice in particular fields can help them to achieve a particular goal or work out how political, economic or sociological context can affect practice.

A variation on this is to use autobiography, to tell the story of an individual in the first person. Autobiographies can be real or fictitious, and set in the past, present or future. They can be written as an imagined piece written by a person famous in the subject, or about someone who worked in the area who didn't become famous, or about themselves as an aspiring member of the discipline.

Level

In general, this kind of assignment is suitable for introductory levels to help students to situate themselves in the discipline; for levels 5–7 it might work better if students are asked to construct a fictitious biography (e.g. of a service user) or to link the experiences of the subject to current practice.

In history or creative writing, this might be a task for higher levels, but in most other subjects it is likely to be an introductory task as the level of analysis will be lower.

Indicative learning outcomes

On completion of this task, students will be able to:

- Describe the life and work of a key historical figure in [the discipline] in relation to the social and political context of the day
- Identify the challenges of being a service user in [the profession] in the period [select time period, which could be in the future]
- Visualise their own future career in [the profession] with consideration of the potential benefits and challenges

Key information

You could ask students to prepare a real biography of a person working in a particular field or ask them to produce a composite or fictitious biography of a person doing a particular job. Autobiography encourages students to reflect on themselves, usually in relation to the course material. For instance, students on a vocationally-oriented course such as social work, physiotherapy or engineering might be asked to reflect on events or experiences which have helped them to develop in those professional areas and identify with the profession. They could also be asked to project themselves forward into the kinds of experiences they expect to have as they progress in their professions. Students in less vocational subjects could be asked to reflect on their own life experiences and life plans and how these are linked to the discipline. What have they learned from the subject, or what tools from the discipline have they applied to other elements of their lives?

Student choice

You can provide a list of potential subjects or allow students to identify their own. If they are finding their own subjects, then you may wish to set the parameter of the search – in what way should the subject be related to the topic of study? Should the subject be celebrated for working in the discipline? Could they be an ordinary person who does a particular job, or has lived with a particular condition or in a country or part of a country, or has a certain approach to life?

Allowing students to choose a subject gives them more ownership of the assignment and can lead to a wider range, which might prove to be more inclusive – for instance, they could be encouraged to find out more about people with different characteristics.

Suitability for groups

This is probably best as an individual task, although it can be done by a pair. It isn't a good group activity, as there is a limited range of roles for this kind of task and the final submission needs to be a coherent piece without variations in style.

Submission size

You might ask for 1,500 words for a fairly descriptive introductory piece, or 2,000–2,500 words at a higher level with some more sophisticated links to the subject material. Alternative formats could be negotiated: 10 minutes of an audio or video file at lower levels, or 15 minutes for higher levels, for instance.

Timing

This is a good introductory task to raise awareness and generate enthusiasm about the possibilities of working in the discipline or profession.

Inclusive practice

This task offers the opportunity to find out more about individuals and how they have engaged with the discipline or profession, so it is a chance to encourage thinking about diversity, particularly if you offer students a choice of subject. Consider whether this must be a written piece, or whether you could consider a choice of written, audio, video, or drawn submissions. Offering a variety of submission modes can allow students to show their strengths: photographs or drawings could be accepted, or narrated PowerPoint slides, for instance. Alternatives may make this more accessible for students with mild to moderate specific learning disabilities and mean that they don't need to ask for individual adjustments.

You need to be confident that the submission types are comparable in difficulty and that you can mark them using the same criteria.

Avoiding academic misconduct

This type of assignment is relatively unusual, which makes it more difficult to plagiarise. If well-known subjects are used, there is scope for copying, but adding a slant specific to your module should help to reduce this. Encourage personal observations and identification with the subject to encourage personal engagement and enthusiasm. You can put some class time aside to get students to discuss work in progress, so that they are supported to keep on task.

Blog

Description

A blog is an online diary which generally has the characteristics of being regularly updated and visible to a selected group or to a wider audience, with readers usually able to comment on the entries. Blogs can be used to provide a descriptive update of an activity (e.g. a work placement, field trip, or experiment), to explore development of a viewpoint or opinion over a period of time (e.g. in response to ideas presented in the unit), or to communicate complex ideas such as research to a specified audience. While the total contents of the blog may be very interesting, the value of this type of assessment generally lies in the process rather than the outcomes: developing a regular writing habit and responding to feedback.

Level

Simple blogs are useful at levels 3 and 4. If you are using them at higher levels, you will probably want to focus on the reflection on what students have learned by, say, writing in a tone suitable for the general public or for an interest group.

Indicative learning outcomes

On completion of this task, students will be able to:

- Communicate work in progress to [a specific audience] in an accessible way
- Demonstrate the development of a project or idea over a period of time in a way suitable for their peers
- Use the discipline of regular reporting to receive and act on feedback from peers

Key information

The summative assessment could be focused on the content of the blog entries themselves, a reflection on the process of writing the blog and responding to reader comments, or in a reflection on the development achieved by the student over the period of keeping the blog. Students could be asked to make a selection of a certain number of their blog entries for summative assessment, accompanied by a short explanation of the reasons for the choice of these entries.

Blogs offer opportunities for peer assessment, both formative and summative, and you can build this into the course planning – for instance, students can be asked to comment meaningfully on at least two other blogs written by their peers or to reflect on differences in approach between individuals given the same brief. Students early in their Bachelor's (first cycle) course might be assessed on their ability to sustain the activity over the period required, the writing style, and the relevance of the content to the target audience. At higher levels, you might expect more reflection on the process of recording, interpretation of the student's own observations in the field or in class, and less description of activity.

Most managed learning environments provide a tool for student blogs which would be accessible to fellow course members. Externally hosted blogs that are available to the general public need to be monitored carefully if they are to be used for course-related activity. In all cases, students need to be briefed on acceptable use of online commentary and reminded that the usual rules of academic writing and commenting apply.

Student choice

You can offer choice over the subject of the whole blog and/or individual entries, as well as over the format of the blog and the intended audience.

Suitability for groups

Yes: students could write alternate entries individually, or as teams. Your expectations for the length and depth of blog entries would of course be higher if groups are working on the blog together. You can give a mark to the whole group for the whole blog, or to individuals for their own sections.

Submission size

You can specify a minimum number of entries to be completed during the module, in the same way as for a portfolio. The length of any reflective element will depend on its weighting in relation to the entries themselves.

Timing

The entries should be completed during the period of the module or practical activity or work placement, with any reflective element being submitted at the end.

Inclusive practice

A blog can allow students to put a personal slant on their work, highlighting what they bring to a project or experience or to the disciplinary area, and how they have managed the excitement and challenges of what they are doing in their studies.

Avoiding academic misconduct

If the blog is regularly updated with topical material, the student may develop a personal style which will make copying more obvious. Discussion of work in progress, and how the blog is received by readers, in class sessions can also help to ensure that the work is the student's own.

Case study

Description

There are two possibilities under this heading: to use a case study which you or someone else has produced to demonstrate students' ability to analyse information, or to ask students to produce a case study which could be used with their peers or with students working at lower levels. The former type is more common and more controllable, but the latter allows for synthesis of the material used on the course and creativity.

Level

Teacher-generated case studies can be used at all levels, as you can make them more complex as students develop. Asking students to develop their own is more suitable for higher levels.

Indicative learning outcomes

On completion of this task, students will be able to:

- Make recommendations to [a defined audience] based on an analysis of data from a situation in [subject area]
- Analyse relevant data about [subject area] to identify causes of [situation from subject area]

Key information

Case studies of real or fictional situations require students to analyse situations in the context of academic theory and evaluate actual outcomes or make their own recommendations for action in that situation. You can base case studies on publicly available documents, such as financial statements, court reports, historical records, medical reports, company policies, newspaper articles and so on, or you can make up realistic fictional versions. The most common outcome for case study activity is a report which reflects the way in which conclusions would be presented in a similar real situation. You can also add a short account which explains how they went about the task.

Asking students to prepare case studies of their own can be useful as it gives them insight into the range of information which needs to be collected and collated to get a full picture of a situation. You can take this a stage further by involving them in the use of the case studies with other groups. The main disadvantage of this type of assessment is that it may be difficult to predict and control the outcomes, which can make marking time-consuming or make the assignment stressful for students. However, this is the case for all open-ended or creative assignments, and both issues can be mitigated by providing clear guidance and assessment criteria.

Student choice

You can offer a choice of case studies from different companies, organisations, or situations. With the option of creating a case study, you can encourage students to identify and explore data of their own choosing.

Suitability for groups

Case studies lend themselves well to group work as it is possible for work to be divided up, either by individuals taking on roles which reflect those which might be adopted in real situations, or by dividing up the research and analysis.

Submission size

In most cases, a realistic workplace-style report will be requested for this kind of assignment, comprising an executive summary and then a more detailed report. The total length, including appendices, should reflect the number of students working on it and the credit rating of the unit.

Timing

Case studies can be set at any point in a programme. Because they represent a realistic work situation, they can make an engaging early task for new students, to help them see how their studies relate to professional lives. Equally, they work well towards the end of a programme to allow students to prepare something realistic that they can discuss at interviews.

Inclusive practice

You can allow students to focus on a situation they are particularly interested in, to identify their own organisations or policies to study, and to suggest examples from their own experiences, perhaps in other countries with which they are familiar. The format of the final report can also be selected by the student to suit their own preferred style: written, video, poster, or leaflet, for instance.

Avoiding academic misconduct

If you use a new, topical case study each year, then plagiarism is unlikely to be a problem. The potential for cheating can also be reduced by asking for regular short progress reports.

Competence portfolio

Description

The portfolio is useful for encouraging regular engagement with the course materials and ensuring that students have grasped something before moving on. Students put together a portfolio of evidence of how required learning outcomes have been achieved. Students may be given a series of tasks to complete at intervals during the module or work placement, or they could put together a selection of evidence which they have chosen themselves. Students usually present a portfolio which provides evidence to support how they can perform in particular roles or tasks.

Level

Competence can be assessed at all levels.

Indicative learning outcomes

On completion of this task, students will be able to:

- Present a coherent summary of their professional achievements in relation to [professional standards, or named topic]
- Demonstrate their ability to carry out tasks in a professional environment
- Plan and carry out a variety of professional tasks in [topic]

Key information

The list of skills for which students may claim achievement needs to be clear: it could include team work, initiative-taking, problem-solving, time management, communications, critical incident analysis, and planning. If the portfolio is linked to a professional accreditation, the list of required tasks will probably be prescribed, but if you are designing it yourself, you could ask for evidence of completion of certain tasks, descriptions of situations encountered, contemporaneous notes taken by the students, reports or notes taken by practice colleagues, and evidence of outcomes. If students are completing a series of set tasks, then it will be simplest to use proformas to indicate, when, and where the task was completed, what was done, and how competence was confirmed.

Practice assessments are usually carried out in real or very realistic situations, so some thought needs to be given to how these are set up if they are not in a work placement.

In terms of marking, a competence portfolio will consist of a series of elements which will often only be graded as pass/fail. The options for giving a grade are:

- All tasks must be passed: portfolio is given a pass with no grade attached
- At least X% of tasks must be passed: portfolio is given a grade depending on the percentage of tasks successfully completed
- Individual tasks are graded and the portfolio is given a grade which reflects the average grade across all tasks (see analytical marking schemes, Chapter 6)

The grading system may be determined by an external professional body. Sometimes individual elements will be signed off as they are completed; this could be done by a colleague in the workplace, or by a teacher. You will need to take this into account when planning marking and moderation, and ensure that the practice tutor or colleague is familiar with university regulations and checks so that everyone has confidence in the procedure.

Suitability for groups

Competence portfolios assess individual ability to carry out a series of authentic professional tasks. It would be difficult to set up a suitable situation which allows for reliable and comprehensive assessment of a group, so this is most suitable for assessment of individuals.

Submission size

Students need guidance on the quantity of material to be included, otherwise the workload for both students and staff may quickly become unacceptable. For professional qualifications, portfolio size may be well established through custom and practice, which would give you a starting point. If you are designing something new, then think about how long it takes a typical student to learn, practise, and demonstrate a new skill. Using the rule of thumb of about 25% of module time dedicated to assignment preparation, how many such tasks can be reasonably completed?

Timing

Competence portfolios are usually produced over a period of time and submitted at the end of a module or course.

Inclusive practice

Competence portfolios tend to have a tightly prescribed format which means that you may have little flexibility in relation to the provision of choice. If that is the case, it may be necessary to make accommodations for different student situations, in discussion with students, workplace colleagues, technical staff, and disability advisors, where appropriate.

Avoiding academic misconduct

Portfolios may look very similar, particularly if proformas are used for each task or skill. If competence is being signed off by a teacher or by a workplace supervisor, then you can be sure that students have completed the task. If students are making their own claims for competence, regular discussion and review of the draft portfolios will help you to link the individual to the work directly.

Essay

Description

An essay is a piece of structured writing which is used to develop an argument or opinion in a logical way. Essays are probably the most commonly used form of academic assessment for both coursework and examinations. They are usually presented to students in the form of a one or two sentence brief; such briefs need to be carefully constructed to ensure that what is expected of the student is clear and so that it is possible to mark the essays objectively.

Level

Essays can be set at any level of study. Your expectations will evidently depend on the level of the students. For novice students, you might focus on the structure of the work and developing their writing skills, but for students nearing the end of their studies you will be looking at their ability to create persuasive arguments.

Indicative learning outcomes

On completion of this task, students will be able to:

- Create an argument to persuade [a specified audience] about [topics in the subject area]
- Compare different aspects of [the topic]

Key information

Essays can be used to encourage students to focus on a topic in more depth than was possible in lectures, to construct an argument in the discipline, to synthesise the breadth of the material covered in the course in application to one problem, to form a hypothesis on using what was learned in the course or some combination of the above.

Essays are often set using a one sentence brief. Consider how open-ended you want this sentence to be, particularly at lower levels. If you use the one-sentence approach, you might qualify it with more detailed instructions about context, such as 'which of the approaches is more likely to result in success' or 'evaluate the impact of this statement on a recent development in the profession' to make it clearer what you are looking for. At lower levels, you could provide more clues about what you are expecting by asking for a structured essay, with broad headings about what should be included.

Student choice

Consider whether this must be a written piece, or whether you could consider a choice of written, audio, video, photographic, or drawn submissions. Alternatives may make this more accessible for students with mild to moderate specific learning disabilities and result in a richer range of submissions.

You also need to decide whether you want to offer students a choice of essay title, to allow them to focus on a topic or approach which suits their own interests and skills. You need to be confident that the titles and submission types are comparable in difficulty and that you can mark them using the same criteria.

Suitability for groups

Essays are traditionally individual pieces of work, as they are intended to allow students to develop and present a personal perspective and opinion. They could be undertaken by a pair or small group, if you want to focus more on process.

Submission size

Essays are a very familiar task for most people working in universities and this can make it challenging to do things differently. It is reasonable for students to expect assignments with the same name to have similar length, but there is considerable difference between disciplines – science subjects which set essays often expect more concise pieces than the equivalent in humanities, and there could be a similar case for having different purposes for different assignments on the same course. Custom and practice will be a powerful guide, so look around at what is done in other institutions as well as your own, but don't be afraid to deconstruct tradition and set your own. Ask existing students how long they spend on the traditional-length essays to give you some idea about workload. Generally, you can set longer essays at higher levels.

Timing

Towards the end of a module when students have engaged with most of the material and have been able to develop an argument.

Inclusive practice

Essays are traditionally written and this can be challenging for students with mild to moderate specific learning difficulties, who may find processing the written word particularly problematic. You can offer choice over the topic and encourage students to bring their previous knowledge and experience to bear, perhaps considering the use of sources written in languages other than English if the students have the skills to bring those into an essay (but see next section for things to watch out for in that situation).

Avoiding academic misconduct

There is likely to be plenty of similar material available to students, as essays are so commonly used and in certain core disciplinary areas there is a limit to the number of original topics one can create. This is a powerful incentive for contract cheating sites that sell essays. You can reduce the plagiarism potential by relating the essay title to topical issues, asking for essay plans at various stages in the term and discussing the content of the essay in seminars.

Encouraging students to use sources unfamiliar to you may make it difficult for you to be certain it is their own work, so consider asking for a short (one paragraph) explanation of each resource used which isn't in your own library or language, and indicating that you keep the right to have an oral assessment if necessary, if this is allowed within your regulations.

Event

Description

Asking students to organise an event to which a number of other people are invited can be a good way of allowing them to demonstrate that they can synthesise disciplinary knowledge and a variety of transferable skills, such as time and project management and team working. Events could be feasible in most disciplinary areas: you could think about public consultations, displays of student work, performances, exhibitions, awards, local history club meetings, debates, film shows, research reporting, mini-conferences, lectures from external speakers, sports competitions or displays, and so on.

Level

This is a complex assignment suitable for level 5–7.

Indicative learning outcomes

On completion of this task, students will be able to:

• Organise [type of event] for [defined audience or participants] with consideration of [context]

Key information

This assessment is suitable for you to manage if you have ever been involved in organising an event of any kind yourself, and probably best avoided if you haven't ever done this. It doesn't have to have been an academic event; the process is similar whatever the context: school concert, charity sale, car wash, award presentation evening – anything, really.

You would need to decide whether the event planning could be done purely as a plan (an imaginary event) or will be followed through to an actual event. In either case, students may need quite a lot of support with this kind of task. At level 5, you might need to give a lot of guidance about how a successful event is planned, what steps need to be taken, and you might also need to check plans at regular intervals and to ask them about contingencies. Students might get involved in co-organising an academic event with you and colleagues (e.g. a series of seminars or a one-day conference) to shadow the process and learn about what needs to be done. It would be prudent to start with the formative task of organising a small event or making the planning elements formative, so that they receive feedback before proceeding to a real event.

There are various ways of assessing the event itself, which will depend on the learning outcomes for the unit. You could judge the event in the same sort of way as you might assess a presentation, using a standard feedback sheet. You might not evaluate the event itself, but expect a written report from the group on the process of organising it and their analysis of its success, and mark that alone. If so, are you going to assess the process alone, or do you also want to evaluate their reflections on the process of organising the event rather than its success? How much will feedback from other participants in the event count? If you want to assess their ability to work in groups, will you take into account their peer assessments or will you judge this by the outcomes?

As with all event-based marking, consider whether you need to have two people making the assessment judgements, or whether you can sample marking by having a moderator attend different events. Usually these activities are large enough to make it feasible to have two or more assessors at the event.

Event organisation is an excellent type of assignment for students who have good analytical and organisational skills, as they can potentially do well even if their skills of written expression are less good.

Student choice

This task has a lot of choice embedded in it: how many people, venue, how to promote the event, whether to have catering and if so, what it will be, and so on. You might actually want to restrict student choices about every element of the event in order to speed up decision-making. Make it clear you aren't looking for an idealised event, but one which they think will work for the intended participants, so that they bring their own views to the planning.

Suitability for groups

Organising an event should always be done in groups as there are a number of roles which need to be undertaken: it would be difficult for an individual to complete all of the tasks successfully, even for a small event. Members of the group will need to select or be allocated different roles If the ability to work in a group is being assessed, then the group could also complete a short submission which explains how roles were allocated and how each contributed to the finished event. They could also peer assess each other's contributions to the task.

Submission size

The size of the event will depend on the context, of course, and the group sizes need to be scaled up depending on the event. You might expect a pair of people to be able to organise a small local event for 5–10 people, with minimal catering, and to need a group of 10 to organise an evening social event for up to 100 people. Your own experience of organising events would need to be a guide.

Timing

Organising events takes time and should be scheduled for the end of a module.

Inclusive practice

With this kind of assignment, there are many opportunities to let students demonstrate what they bring with them to their studies; they can choose styles of event or catering which reflect their preferences and experiences, they can bring in cultural figures they admire, they can involve members of their communities. Talk to them about what interests them and see how much they can bring in.

A big event is a stressful thing to organise, especially if large numbers of participants are expected. You will need to provide a lot of support in terms of talking through what will happen and how to manage unforeseen circumstances and changes of plan.

Avoiding academic misconduct

It would be difficult to copy any element of the event itself in any meaningful way, so plagiarism should not be a problem. The report should be personalised to the event, so it would be unlikely to be something which would be copied or where a contract cheater could do a good job.

Poster

Description

Posters are a well-established way of communicating information, particularly at scientific conferences. In that context, posters can be used as a way of initiating discussion on early results and encouraging discussion and debate that will help with subsequent research. In order to be effective, posters need to catch the attention, summarise a few ideas succinctly, and identify the main issues for debate, discussion or refinement. Like oral presentations, they offer an opportunity for students to present their work to others and to receive rapid feedback from a wider range of people, because you can involve the whole class in feedback, as well as inviting in other members of staff to get a snapshot of progress and interact usefully with students without putting an onerous marking burden on colleagues.

Level

Posters can be used at all levels, with the sophistication of the content increasing as students move through the levels.

Indicative learning outcomes

On completion of this task, students will be able to:

- Synthesise the results of research into a format suitable for presentation to [a specified audience]

Key information

A poster is designed that can either be submitted as a digital file, or you can plan for all of the posters to be displayed on a particular day, on which the student will talk about their own poster and answer questions. A poster event can be digital or in person, and it means that feedback can be collected from the whole class or a small subgroup can comment on each poster. You can also involve a team of teachers in marking the displays, making the event more significant and even fun. This gives students an opportunity to demonstrate and test out their ideas in a supportive atmosphere without a huge marking burden being incurred. Usually, it's an enjoyable experience and everyone gets a lot out of it.

A key decision is whether you are marking artistic or presentational skills as well as the contents of the poster. This will depend on the learning outcomes you have. Designing and presenting posters is an important skill for practising scientists, so you might want to include presentation skills in your outcomes. For other subjects, the content may be the only thing you want to assess.

With large classes it can be logistically difficult to present the posters, but no more so than organising oral presentations. The session needs to be planned carefully; one way is to divide the poster presenters into two or three groups. One group stands by its posters while the tutor(s) and the other groups tour the room, talking to the students about the individual posters. After a set time the groups swap round so that another group stands by the posters while the first group gets to go round the others, and so on. You then need to build in time to give verbal feedback and agree grades.

Students may not have encountered this kind of assessment before and will need to be briefed on the task and resources available to them, such as a reprographics service, if the posters are being printed and displayed. You will need to book a suitable room where the posters can be put up and viewed comfortably, and provide material for displaying the posters.

Student choice

You can offer choice over the topic and the style of the poster.

Suitability for groups

This is suitable for a group task, particularly as there are different roles which can be adopted (data collection, analysis, design) which contribute to the final product.

Submission size

You can specify a size of poster (e.g. A1) and a maximum amount of text (e.g. 500 words) and then leave the rest to the students. There are plenty of templates available online.

Timing

If you want students to use the poster to familiarise themselves with a topic and present to their peers, then this is a good task for early in the programme. If they are going to synthesise a piece of research they have carried out, then it should be set later on.

Inclusive practice

Posters can be a way for students to show their individuality. Depending on the topic area, you can encourage them to bring in information and images from their own interests and experiences. Students who suffer from anxiety may find the poster session challenging, but on the other hand, it may be less difficult than a more formal oral presentation: everyone is in the room with their own poster, and answering questions about the poster can be an informal process. Talk to students about what is going to happen and how you expect it to work, and encourage them to ask questions.

Avoiding academic misconduct

If you use topical subjects, plagiarism is more difficult. The amount of text on a poster is minimal, which may make it more difficult to detect changes of style, but if you build in the time to ask questions about each poster at an event, then you will be able to probe students' understanding of the work. It will be particularly important to remind students about copyright restrictions on the use of images and point them to sources of free images.

Project or dissertation

Description

A project or dissertation is usually a large piece of work, set towards the end of a course, which allows students to build on learning from the whole programme, and show that they can collect data, analyse it, and produce a report.

Level

Projects and dissertations are usually set at level 6 or 7 to allow students to bring together learning from the whole course.

Indicative learning outcomes

On completion of this task, students will be able to:

- Design a research project to investigate [topic area]
- Carry out a research project to investigate [topic area]
- Present the findings of a research project to [a defined audience]

Key information

Projects and dissertations can use primary and/or secondary sources as their main evidence. If the student is designing an experiment to collect primary data, you will need to check safety and they may need to get ethical approval for the work. This needs to be planned in to the time available for the project.

It would be usual for a named teacher to supervise the project or dissertation, and to meet regularly with the student to monitor progress and ensure milestones are achieved. You will find it useful to have an outline for these milestones in the assignment brief, to give everyone a clear structure for working on the project.

Project briefs can be generated from the research interests in the department, or from external sources such as professional or industry contacts. Live project briefs, which are generated by potential employers, are commonly used in art schools, and can be very motivating for students. They can be linked to competitions with prizes such as the chance to have a product made up in a factory, or to be presented at an industry show. These prizes would be additional to the usual marking and feedback process, which would still need to be implemented in order to satisfy quality assurance requirements.

Student choice

Consider whether this must be a written piece, or whether you could consider a choice of written, audio, video, photographic, or drawn submissions. Alternatives may make this more accessible for students with mild to moderate specific learning disabilities and result in a richer range of submissions.

The nature of a project or dissertation is that students will make choices about how they work on the topic, select literature and approach the analysis and creation of the final report or product. You need to be confident that the titles and submission types are comparable in difficulty and that you can mark them using the same criteria.

Suitability for groups

Projects and dissertations can be undertaken by pairs or groups. As these are usually high-stakes assessments, you will need to set ground rules and make it clear how groups should manage their work and deal with any difficulties. The allocation of marks also needs to be very clear.

Submission size

As with essays, it is reasonable for students to expect assignments with the same name to have similar length, but there is considerable difference between disciplines. Custom and practice will be a powerful guide, so look around at what is done in other institutions as well as your own, but don't be afraid to deconstruct tradition and set your own. Ask existing students how long they spend on their projects to give you some idea about workload.

Timing

Towards the end of a course when students have engaged with most of the material and can put together their skills in finding sources, analysing material, designing data collection, managing results, and drawing conclusions or producing artefacts.

Inclusive practice

Projects and dissertations are high-stakes assignment tasks that may cause anxiety. You can offer choice over the topic and encourage students to bring their previous knowledge and experience to bear, perhaps considering the use of sources written in languages other than English if the students have the skills to bring those into their work. You can help students by making the stages of the project very clear, and checking in with them regularly to ensure they are on task.

Avoiding academic misconduct

Plagiarism is more difficult with an original project when you are checking in with the student regularly to review progress, but it isn't impossible. Be prepared to ask questions about the project or dissertation throughout the period of work. Encouraging students to use sources unfamiliar to you may make it difficult for you to be certain it is their own work, so consider asking for a short (one paragraph) explanation of each resource used which isn't in your own library or language, and indicating that you keep the right to have an oral assessment if necessary, if this is allowed within your regulations.

Synthesis portfolio or patchwork text

Description

This kind of portfolio is used for building up skills or knowledge in smaller sections over the period of a unit and then seeing how students reflect on their progress. Students are usually given a series of tasks to complete at intervals during the unit. At the end of the unit, a selection, or all, of the tasks are submitted for summative assessment, together with a reflective account. These tasks might be submitted for formative assessment and feedback from the unit team. The original formative tasks may have been improved by the student for the final assessment, or the originals can be submitted. The task is sometimes called a 'patchwork' as the reflective account 'stitches' the separate activities together into a coherent whole.

The portfolio is useful for encouraging regular engagement with the course materials and ensuring that students have grasped something before moving on. There is a slower build to the final summative assessment and the planning stages can be built into the usual student activities for the unit; assessment is integrated throughout the unit. It can also develop the skills of revision and improvement in response to feedback.

Level

This portfolio is suitable at any level, with more expected from the depth of reflection at higher levels.

Indicative learning outcomes

On completion of this task, students will be able to:

- Reflect on a period of learning in [a particular context] in relation to [disciplinary topic]
- Identify key aspects of professional development in [a particular context] in relation to their own future plans

Key information

This task is useful for encouraging regular engagement with the course materials and ensuring that students have grasped something before moving on. There is a slower build to the final summative assessment and the planning stages can be built into the usual student activities for the unit; assessment is integrated throughout the unit. The task is sometimes called a 'patchwork' as the reflective account 'stitches' the separate activities together into a coherent whole. Some or all of the tasks might be submitted for formative feedback from the unit team, which can also develop the skills of revision and improvement in response to feedback. The original formative tasks may have been improved by the student for the final submission, or the originals can be submitted together with the reflective account which explains what the student has learned from their feedback.

There may be an issue about workload if the marking of the formative work is not properly factored into the unit planning. This may be reduced a little by using generic feedback for the formative stages, but students may find it harder to improve the individual patches or pieces using generic feedback.

When you are planning, remember that students may choose not to submit any or all of the formative tasks, so that there may be some who only submit summatively at the end of the unit. You should make it clear what the deadlines are for submitting formative work, and that you won't be able to give feedback after these times – otherwise you may receive a lot of formative tasks just before the summative assignment deadline.

Student choice

Students can be given choice over the selection of entries for the portfolio and the format.

Suitability for groups

Yes, students can combine and share their activities as long as the reflective account shows how all the pieces have contributed to further learning.

Submission size

The production and maintenance of a portfolio can be time-consuming, and this would normally be taken into account when considering the length of each individual element and the reflective. You need to decide whether you want to see all of the work that students have completed over the term, or a selection of the tasks. If it is a selection, will you choose which items are submitted (say, the lab reports from weeks 3, 7 and 9), or will you leave the choice to students (for instance, submit the four article summaries which best demonstrate your progress over the term)? You could make it time-based, and ask for one piece of evidence per week of the course.

The answer will depend on whether you want to focus mostly on regular performance and acquisition of essential skills, or personal development across the module, and this will be linked to the unit learning outcomes. Make it very clear what you are expecting to see in terms of size, and if there are any penalties for submitting too much, or you may receive many appendices which you won't have time to assess properly.

Timing

Synthesis portfolios need to be produced over a period of time and submitted at the end of a module or course.

Inclusive practice

A reflective piece gives students an opportunity to explain what they have brought to the tasks and how their unique skills and knowledge have developed during the module. You can also encourage discussion of any particular challenges they may have faced and how these were overcome.

Avoiding academic misconduct

Portfolios may look very similar, but the development of a piece of assessment over time reduces opportunities for plagiarism, as does the addition of a personal reflective piece to explain the selection of material.

Examinations and tests (time-constrained assessments)

Examinations are assessments which are undertaken under controlled conditions such as a restricted choice of questions, supervision by assessors or invigilators, and a constraint on the time available to complete the task. They can be taken in-person or online. Examinations may be selected for one or more of the following principal reasons:

1   To test knowledge and comprehension over the whole course, because students may not know what is in the questions, they need to prepare across the whole curriculum, even though they will only answer a certain number of questions.
2   To prevent cheating, since the students are supervised while the assignment is being carried out.
3   To ensure that all students complete the assignment task under the same conditions.

Some kinds of examinations are also used because they are more manageable for large numbers of students, for instance those which can be marked by computer.

There are some general points to consider about all three of these reasons. First, it is important to consider what knowledge can reasonably be assessed in a time-constrained task: students will be able to reproduce information and apply it to fairly simple situations similar to those they have seen before, but they will not have time for reflection and synthesis of complex ideas. Second, it is impossible to rule out cheating completely: it may be reduced by the presence of supervision, but someone who is determined to gain an unfair advantage will find a way. Third, the existence of the controlled conditions may have the undesirable effect of making it more difficult for some students to demonstrate their achievement of the learning outcomes, because they find the constraints so stressful. While different types of examination will have these limitations to different extents, it is worth bearing them in mind when deciding whether or not to control the conditions of your assessment tasks.

Universities usually have detailed regulations covering the management of examinations, including supervision of student behaviour to ensure that nobody is cheating. On-campus examinations are supervised by invigilators in the room. Online, webcams may be used to monitor students, and there is technology, called **remote proctoring** software, which can be used to track student movements and the ways that the student's computer is used. You may not feel that you have much influence over institution-wide regulations which relate to invigilation, but you should be aware of them and contribute to discussion where possible. On-campus invigilation is fairly well established and is usually well accepted, but the same is not always true for online monitoring. Remote proctoring, particularly if carried out in an automated way, can be intrusive and discriminatory. This is usually because algorithms may not take into account behaviours which a human observer would realise to be innocuous (for instance, staring up at the ceiling for inspiration, or the existence of a tic giving rise to unexpected head movements, or a medical need for frequent restroom breaks). The software may also require students to share views of their personal living conditions, which may make them feel uncomfortable.

Unseen examination

Description

This kind of assessment almost needs no introduction, as most people will have heard the phrase '*you may now turn your paper over*' at some time in their educational career. An unseen exam is a time-constrained assessment task, presented to students for the first time at the beginning of the assessment. Unseen exams may be taken in an examination room or online, and are usually supervised by invigilators or proctors. They can be hand-written or typed onto a computer, or can involve the completion of an individual task, such as writing computer code. The unseen examination format is sometimes required by professional bodies.

Level

Unseen examinations can be set at any level of higher education.

Indicative learning outcomes

On completion of this task, students will be able to:

- Describe the characteristics of [a set of knowledge from the discipline]
- Identify the major theories of [topic area] and give examples of their use in [range of contexts]
- Identify the important elements of a case study and produce a development plan

Key information

The traditional unseen exam consists of a series of essay questions or of scientific or mathematical problems. The wording of the questions will reflect whether you want students to demonstrate recall of the course material under examination conditions (using phrasing such as 'describe', or to apply what they have learned to novel situations and problems (using 'evaluate', 'analyse' and 'solve'). It can be difficult to do both of these things thoroughly under time-constrained conditions.

Student choice

There is unlikely to be choice over whether, how, or when to take the examination, although students are often given a choice over which questions they answer. This choice may mean that in fact the conditions of the examination are not the same for everyone, as it can be difficult to be certain that all questions are equally difficult.

Suitability for groups

Written examinations are not suitable for groups.

Submission size

The size of the submission is usually indicated by the duration of the examination, with no suggestions about how much should be written or produced in this time. You may have an idea about what you are expecting in terms of length, and it would be useful to share this with students. The usual rule of thumb for an exam question is that students should be able to sit and write the answer in half the time available for the question (the other half of the time being for thinking and planning). In a two-hour exam, students might be able to write 1,500–2,000 words in total, but this is very variable depending on discipline and level.

Timing

Examinations can be set at any time after a certain amount of knowledge has been taught, but, for practical reasons, such as availability of large, secure spaces and of invigilators, they are often scheduled at the end of a module or course.

Inclusive practice

Unseen exams test the ability to work under a time constraint and can be very stressful for students. They may favour students with particular personalities and previous experiences of success in similar situations, and disadvantage students who are prone to anxiety. It is also worth considering whether they achieve your intended purposes for the task: unseen exams are an artificial situation which students are unlikely to encounter outside education. For these reasons, they are best used as part of a varied assessment strategy to allow students to demonstrate their ability in a range of situations.

Students who need extra time for writing, or who have difficulty in hand-writing and need to type their assignments, will need arrangements to be made in advance. Sometimes, students with severe anxiety may need to take their examination in a room apart from other students. There also need to be arrangements for students to use the bathroom when needed. These arrangements will usually be made by professional services teams in the university on a consistent basis for all courses, but if you are managing an unseen examination in your own classes, you will need to think about these things.

Avoiding academic misconduct

There are unlikely to be plagiarism issues with an unseen exam, although students with excellent recall may be able to use the words of others to answer questions; these would be difficult and time-consuming to detect when papers are hand-written. Restricting the items available in the examination room will make it difficult to copy from pre-prepared notes of any kind.

There are still ways to cheat, though: identification through identity cards may not always be easy for an invigilator, students may be able to see what others are writing, if they are in an examination room, or find ways to look things up in an online situation.

Seen examination

Description

A seen examination is a time-constrained assessment task, presented to students at some time in advance of the assessment. The actual exam is still taken under strict conditions, with no external material allowed into the exam room and a time limit for completing the answers, although a seen examination can be combined with an open-book examination, in which you allow students to bring in books or folders.

A variation on the seen examination may be to provide some material ahead of the examination, such as a case study, and to say that questions will be set around that case study.

Seen examinations are sometimes used to reduce student anxiety about exams or to allow the inclusion of more complex analytical questions which need some preparation.

Level

Seen examinations can be set at any level of higher education.

Indicative learning outcomes

These are the same as those for an unseen exam, but you can add more complex contexts. On completion of this task, students will be able to:

- Describe the characteristics of [a set of knowledge from the discipline]
- Identify the major theories of [topic area] and give examples of their use in [range of contexts]
- Identify the important elements of a case study and produce a development plan

Key information

The timing of the release of the question(s) is important. If you want students to think about the question throughout the module, then it could be released right at the beginning of the module and referred to regularly during the course. If you want students to work to a time constraint, as they might have to in the workplace, then you could release the question 1–6 weeks before the exam.

Student choice

There is unlikely to be choice over whether, how, or when to take the examination, although students are often given a choice over which questions they answer. This choice may mean that in fact the conditions of the examination are not the same for everyone, as it can be difficult to be certain that all questions are equally difficult.

Suitability for groups

Written examinations are not suitable for groups.

Submission size

The size of the submission is usually indicated by the duration of the examination, with no suggestions about how much should be written or produced in this time. You may have an idea about what you are expecting in terms of length, and it would be useful to share this with students. The usual rule of thumb for an exam question is that students should be able to sit and write the answer in half the time available for the question (the other half of the time being for thinking and planning). In a two-hour exam, students might be able to write 1,500–2,000 words in total, but this is very variable depending on discipline and level.

With a seen exam, there would be less reflection required on the day, so you might increase your expectations of the length. This would clearly have an effect on the time needed to mark the exams, which needs to be factored in.

Timing

Examinations can be set at any time after a certain amount of knowledge has been taught, but, for practical reasons, such as availability of large, secure spaces and of invigilators, they are often scheduled at the end of a module or course.

Inclusive practice

Seen exams may be less stressful than unseen ones as they allow students to prepare and know what they will be expected to do during the examination. As with unseen exams, it is worth considering whether they achieve your intended purposes for the task: these exams are an artificial situation which students are unlikely to encounter outside education. For these reasons, they are best used as part of a varied assessment strategy to allow students to demonstrate their ability in a range of situations.

Students who need extra time for writing, or who have difficulty in hand-writing and need to type their assignments, will need arrangements to be made in advance. Sometimes, students with severe anxiety may need to take their examination in a room apart from other students. There also need to be arrangements for students to use the bathroom when needed. These arrangements will usually be made by professional services teams in the university on a consistent basis for all courses, but if you are managing an unseen examination in your own classes, you will need to think about these things.

Avoiding academic misconduct

Plagiarism could possibly be a problem as students with excellent recall may be able to use the words of others to answer questions; such cheating would be difficult and time-consuming to detect if papers are hand-written.

Students will of course be able to discuss the question in advance of the exam, and this may lead to some similarity of answers, just as you might find for a coursework assessment.

Open-book examination

Description

Time-constrained unseen exams where students can bring in books or folders can be useful if you want to test skills in application, analysis, and evaluation, or to present students with new situations or scenarios to be addressed against a deadline.

They can be particularly useful if you want to see how students cope with a particular professional situation without much time to consult widely. They also test students' ability to identify and bring with them the right kind of material: if this is important, make sure it is mentioned in the learning outcomes.

Level

Open-book examinations can be set at any level of higher education, but if the selection of material is complex, then the task may be more suitable for higher levels (5–7).

Indicative learning outcomes

On completion of this task, students will be able to:

- Apply appropriate theories to a situation in professional practice
- Identify the important elements of a case study and produce a development plan using a selection of approaches
- Use relevant reference material to create a suitable response to a client enquiry

Key information

The wording of the questions is very important, and will need to test students' ability to apply available information to a new situation rather than their ability to recall what has been learned on the course. You need to specify in advance what type of material, and how much of it, students can bring in. This could range from one piece of paper to an entire folder they have prepared themselves. Will you allow textbooks, and if so, will you specify which ones and which editions are allowed? If annotations are not permitted, you will need to check everything or provide the books yourselves.

If you have set constraints on the type or volume of material, you need to have procedures in place for checking whether material is acceptable. Students will need clear guidance on how to prepare their materials and themselves for the exam and what the purpose of using the open-book approach is.

Student choice

There is unlikely to be choice over whether, how, or when to take the examination, although students are often given a choice over which questions they answer, and they may be able to choose what items they bring to the room.

Suitability for groups

Written examinations are not suitable for groups.

Submission size

The size of the submission is usually indicated by the duration of the examination, with no suggestions about how much should be written or produced in this time. You may have an idea about what you are expecting in terms of length, and it would be useful to share this with students. The usual rule of thumb for an exam question is that students should be able to sit and write the answer in half the time available for the question (the other half of the time being for thinking and planning). In a two-hour exam, students might be able to write 1,500–2,000 words in total, but this is very variable depending on discipline and level.

With an unseen open-book exam, students need time to use the material, so you might decrease your expectations of the length.

Timing

Examinations can be set at any time after a certain amount of knowledge has been taught, but, for practical reasons, such as availability of large, secure spaces and of invigilators, they are often scheduled at the end of a module or course.

Inclusive practice

Open-book exams may be less stressful than unseen ones as they allow students to prepare and know what they will be expected to do during the examination, but the worry of not knowing the questions may still be significant for some students. You can combine the open-book format with a seen question. As with all exams, it is worth considering whether they achieve your intended purposes for the task: these exams are an artificial situation which students are unlikely to encounter outside education. For these reasons, they are best used as part of a varied assessment strategy to allow students to demonstrate their ability in a range of situations.

Students who need extra time for writing, or who have difficulty in hand-writing and need to type their assignments, will need arrangements to be made in advance. Sometimes, students with severe anxiety may need to take their examination in a room apart from other students. There also need to be arrangements for students to use the bathroom when needed. These arrangements will usually be made by professional services teams in the university on a consistent basis for all courses, but if you are managing an unseen examination in your own classes, you will need to think about these things.

Avoiding academic misconduct

Examinations do not generally carry a risk of plagiarism. However, if students can bring in materials, there is an increased risk. This can be reduced by having topical questions which require analysis and synthesis rather than factual recall, although, as previously discussed, it can be difficult to get much analysis and synthesis into a time-constrained task. If recall is important, then open-book exams are not a good option.

Take-home examination

Description

A take-home examination is a time-constrained assessment task, presented to students at some time in advance of the assessment and completed at home. This kind of task is really a hybrid of coursework and examination: you can think of it either as coursework with a shorter time constraint than usual, or an examination with fewer controls. They are sometimes used to reduce student anxiety about exams, as students have more agency about when they complete it and have access to resources.

Take-home exams were extensively used during the coronavirus pandemic of 2020–2022 as an alternative to unseen examinations taken on-site. This was because there was a sudden shift away from in-person exams for infection control reasons; there was a lack of confidence in the software available to recreate those examination conditions and worries that students would have technical problems which would affect their ability to demonstrate their achievement of learning outcomes. If you are planning for an online exam from the beginning, rather than switching at short notice from a planned in-person exam, you would take these factors into account.

The examination questions are distributed to students and then the completed scripts are returned within a specified period of time. This can be anything from a few hours to some days.

Level

Take-home examinations can be set at all levels.

Indicative learning outcomes

On completion of this task, students will be able to:

- Apply [knowledge from the discipline] to a [defined situation]
- Identify the important elements of [a defined situation] and produce a development plan

Key information

Careful thought is needed about how much time you allow between release of the task description and the submission. For a task which might have taken two hours in an unseen exam, do you allow four hours, eight hours, 24 hours, a week? Obviously, the more time you give, the more work students could do on the task and the more you would need to adjust your expectations of what can be produced. Are you trying to reduce the possibility of technical problems? If so, you should choose a short window (four hours?) and make it clear that you expect students to start on it as soon as it is released, and submit it when between two and four hours have elapsed.

Are you trying to accommodate students working in different time zones? If so, then 24 hours is more reasonable, but some students might work on it for the entire time it is available, giving themselves an advantage. You could say that you expect submission within a certain period of time after the student has accessed the task description, if you have the means to do so. Of course, some students might access the task early and share it with others and you wouldn't be able to identify any advantage that may have been gained by doing this.

The traditional format of the examination can be changed to release questions in the form of short tasks (to test a range of knowledge, as an exam would), to be completed over short, fixed periods, rather than releasing all of the questions at once for a single submission – e.g. one question every two days, with submission of one task being followed by release of the next question.

Student choice

There is unlikely to be choice over whether, how, or when to take the examination, or the format of the submissions, although students are often given a choice over which questions they answer. This choice may mean that in fact the conditions of the examination are not the same for everyone, as it can be difficult to be certain that all questions are equally difficult.

Suitability for groups

It may be possible for you to set a take-home exam for a pair or small group, but it is also unconventional. Carrying out a more controlled assessment for a group can be more stressful than working individually on an exam. If you want to test skills of working in a group, then coursework is better as it allows students to work together over a period of time and then to reflect on the process.

Submission size

The usual rule of thumb for an *unseen* exam question is that students should be able to sit and write the answer in half the time available for the question (the other half of the time being for thinking and planning). In a two-hour exam, students might be able to write 1,500–2,000 words in total, but this is very variable depending on discipline and level. With a take-home exam, you should make it clear how long you expect students to spend on actually answering the question, and ask them to aim for a submission size which reflects this.

Timing

Examinations can be set at any time after a certain amount of knowledge has been taught, but, for practical reasons, such as availability of large, secure spaces and of invigilators, they are often scheduled at the end of a module or course.

Inclusive practice

A take-home exam may be less stressful for some students who find time-constrained exams particularly challenging. Careful thought is needed about how long students have between receiving the paper and submitting their work, to reduce the stress but not to make it a piece of coursework. However, there may be quite a lot of variability in how long students actually spend on it, which is clearly problematic in terms of fairness. This is one of the challenges of a hybrid exam/coursework kind of task.

Students who need help with typing or transcribing their work will need to ensure that they have appropriate support available during the time period set for the exam, or you can consider accepting submissions from them in a different format (e.g. audio).

Avoiding academic misconduct

Students will of course be able to discuss the question in advance of submission, and this may lead to some similarity of answers, just as you might find for a coursework assessment. You can have a pool of questions which are allocated randomly to different students, if you want to reduce similarities.

Objective Structured (Clinical) Examination

Description

An Objective Structured (Clinical) Examination, or OSCE, is typically an examination where students move around between different 'stations', each of which has a short assessment task which will be completed in front of an examiner. They are often used in healthcare courses to assess clinical skills, but they can be used for any subject where you want to test a series of knowledge and practical skills together, in which case they would be OSEs. Possible situations might be in laboratory work or legal case management.

Level

OSCEs test applied skills, so are usually suitable at higher levels, 5–7.

Indicative learning outcomes

On completion of this task, students will be able to:

- Make appropriate decisions about the care of a patient in [context]
- Provide appropriate advice to a client in [context]

Key information

Students would normally arrive at a station and receive a brief, which they can look at before going into the station and beginning the task. Each station needs to be roughly equivalent in difficulty and length, so that you can keep the students moving around the assessments smoothly. For assessments where the student will be interacting with a representative patient or client, actors are often used. If you are working with an actor, you will need to prepare a brief for them too; care needs to be taken to set parameters which are the same for everyone even if the fine detail of the assessment is varied. As with all event-based marking, consider whether you need to have two assessors present who should complete the mark sheet independently before conferring to agree a final grade after the assessment, or whether you can sample the marking with random checks from a moderator.

The 'O' in the name stands for 'objective'; to try to make the marking objective, an analytical marking scheme which is focused on small tasks is very often used, rather than trying to mark a whole piece with a single grade. A clear analytical scheme will also help the examiner to make quick and accurate decisions about the student's performance on that task. Each task may be assessed on a pass/refer basis, or graded. The final mark is usually based on an average of the marks for each task; if some tasks are weighted more heavily than others, you need to let the students know so that they know how much time and effort they need to spend on each one. The examiner usually marks the student's performance on the spot, and then the marks from each station are combined to make a grade for the whole examination.

As with all event-based marking, consider whether you need to have two people at each assessment station, or whether you can sample marking at each station by having a moderator circulating during the examination.

Students may be unfamiliar with this kind of examination, so some formative practice and support for preparation will be needed.

Student choice

One of the reasons for choosing OS(C)Es is to ensure that students can cover a wide range of topics, which means there is unlikely to be choice over the questions. You might give them a little flexibility by discounting the stations on which the student performs worst, so that if they do have a disaster under the exam conditions, they know that it might not count, and they aren't put off trying for the remaining stations.

Suitability for groups

OS(C)Es are usually completed as individuals, but it is possible to design short group tasks if that is better for demonstrating achievement of the learning outcomes, for example, if team work is appropriate.

Submission size

The length of time per task will obviously depend on the type of activity, but around 10 minutes for each task, with the same amount of preparation time, gives time to assess a situation and make some decisions. The number of stations will depend on how many things you have to assess, and the availability of assessors. Students move round from one station to the next, so each station should be set the same length of time to avoid bottlenecks.

Timing

OSCEs can be held in the middle or at the end of a module.

Inclusive practice

Like all time-constrained tasks, this kind of assignment can be stressful; students may find it helpful if you explain exactly what will happen during the presentation and give them opportunities to practise.

If students need to read about the station before going in, then make sure that students with mild to moderate learning disabilities will have enough time; this can affect the planning of the examinations, as students will be rotating around the different stations.

These kinds of tasks are often required for professional accreditation, so you may not be able to offer alternatives for students who are unable to undertake them. If you do have flexibility, you can consider using video case studies which students can replay; they can produce written plans for what they would do, or you can still ask for a live description of this.

Avoiding academic misconduct

As with all examinations, there are unlikely to be plagiarism issues with an unseen OS(C)E. Stations usually test a student's ability to apply their knowledge to a particular situation, rather than testing recall of knowledge, so the chances of plagiarism are further reduced. Oral questioning may be used to explore how students are making their decisions;

a framework for this is recommended, to ensure all examiners are using it equitably. You may want to supervise student movements between stations and ban the use of mobile phones, so that students can't gain an unfair advantage by sharing questions once they have completed a station.

Practical examination

Description

A practical examination tests the student's ability to perform under certain constrained conditions, which may be realistic for certain courses when using specialist equipment, working under pressure, and coping with a selection of variables is required. You can use them in laboratory situations in science, but also for working through protocols or using equipment in other disciplines.

Level

You can design practical examinations for any level of study.

Indicative learning outcomes

On completion of this task, students will be able to:

- Carry out [a procedure] to professional standards using [a range of equipment]
- Analyse [a sample] and report on the findings
- Select the appropriate procedure to test [a range of situations]

Key information

Actual practice situations may be difficult to control for examination purposes, so such assessments are usually set up in the university rather than in practice. Actors may be used to role play if other people are needed in the situation (see also OS(C)Es). The disadvantages of this are that the examination is not precisely the same for all candidates, and care needs to be taken to set parameters which are the same for everyone even if the fine detail of the assessment is varied. A practical examination often has an analytical marking scheme which breaks the skills required into small tasks, each of which is passed or failed, rather than trying to allocate marks based on the level on which the task is carried out. The final mark is usually based on an average of the marks for each task; if some tasks are weighted more heavily than others, you need to let the students know so that they know how much time and effort they need to spend on each one. A rubric will be needed to support decision-making and to provide feedback on the performance of each element of the skill. The examiner usually marks the student performance on the spot, and then the marks from each station are combined to make a grade for the whole examination.

As with all event-based marking, consider whether you need to have two assessors present who should complete the mark sheet independently before conferring to agree a final grade after the assessment, or whether you can sample the marking with random checks from a moderator.

An alternative to observation of performance in an examination is to get the student to write up notes in the way that would be done in a real situation and then to complete the assessment by writing an analysis of the situation and the decision-making process selected, perhaps with a critique of the approach added on for students at higher levels. This approach can also be used for reporting on real-life practice situations. In this case, you would probably choose a holistic scheme.

Student choice

There is unlikely to be choice over whether, how, or when to take the examination, or what is being assessed.

Suitability for groups

It is possible to assess performance in pairs or groups, if you are more focused on the outputs of the practical work. If you want to assess the process of completing the work and using equipment, then the exam should be individual.

Submission size

A rough guide would be to estimate how long it would take an experienced user to complete the practical examination, and then double the time available for the student, taking into account their lesser experience and the influence of nerves.

Timing

Practical examinations can be set at any point in a module once the student has had a chance to practise.

Inclusive practice

Like all time-constrained tasks, this kind of assignment can be stressful; students may find it helpful if you explain exactly what will happen during the presentation and give them opportunities to practise.

Avoiding academic misconduct

Practical examinations which test a student's ability to apply their knowledge to a particular situation, rather than testing recall of knowledge, are unlikely to lead to cheating.

Oral questioning may be used to explore how students are making their decisions; a framework for this is recommended, to ensure all examiners are using it equitably. You may want to supervise student movements between stations and ban the use of mobile phones, so that students cannot gain an unfair advantage by sharing questions once they have completed a station.

Multiple-choice test

Description

A multiple-choice test contains a series of questions. Each question has a *stem* and there is a selection of responses provided to each stem. One or more of the responses is correct; the incorrect responses are known as distractors. Students can choose the response(s) they think are correct. The final grade is achieved by adding up the number of correctly answered questions. Multiple-choice tests are a good way to review coverage of a wide area of knowledge.

Level

You can use multiple-choice examinations at any level, but they are more difficult to use for complex synthesis, so are more common at levels 3–5. In some professional disciplines, such as medicine, they are used to replicate making multiple rapid decisions using specific information which is similar to that which might be found in practice, so they are used at higher levels.

Indicative learning outcomes

On completion of this task, students will be able to:

- Identify the characteristics of [an aspect of the topic area]
- Choose the best options from a selection of professional dilemmas

Key information

A multiple-choice question is formed from a stem which provides the scenario, and a set of possible responses. The stem should be clear enough for students who know the answer to be able to tell you it without looking at the options. Both the stems and the responses need to be concise, so that students can focus quickly on the main purpose of the question. Avoid the use of negatives (such as 'Which of these is not...') as students may be confused about what is actually being asked for.

Each of the possible responses should be plausible, otherwise students will be able to eliminate some of the distractors, in effect reducing the number of options. The 'single best answer' format offers a range of options which have correct elements, from which students have to choose the one which is best. This is the best approach to use when you are testing more than factual recall, and judgement is required.

Usually, all of the questions in a test are of equal difficulty and thus are weighted equally. If you decide to have questions of varying difficulty, they should be weighted differently so that students know that they need to spend longer on higher scoring questions.

Most online assessment software will offer variations on the presentation of the questions: printed responses may be in the form of a list of words or images, and it may be possible to drag and drop selected responses somewhere on a screen. You should be able to choose whether to have one correct answer, or whether students should select any answers which apply, or whether they should put responses into a particular order, such as highest to lowest impact, or the steps of a protocol.

If you are using these tests formatively, you will need to include feedback on each incorrect response; you can also include links to course materials which students can go back to in order to refresh their skills or memories. For summative examinations, students may not receive feedback, but you can think about using generic feedback on any questions which were frequently answered incorrectly, to help them to focus their study in the future.

Writing good multiple-choice questions is challenging and takes time, but can save a lot of marking time at a later stage, even if you take into account that question creation becomes more complex as the level increases. There are numerous online resources which you may find useful for designing multiple-choice tests, and many textbook publishers also make multiple-choice questions available if you adopt the book – but you will need to check them for quality.

You can also consider asking students to write multiple-choice questions as a suitable assignment task. It is challenging, and so can be a way for them to show that they have mastered the topic and possible different interpretations.

Student choice

One of the reasons for choosing multiple-choice questions is to ensure students can cover a wide range of topics, which means that there is unlikely to be choice over the questions. Students will only be able to choose whether to miss out questions they perceive to be particularly difficult.

Suitability for groups

This is usually an individual task. If you did use it with groups or pairs, you would need to build in additional time to discuss and agree on a response. If students are discussing questions, the questions need to be more challenging and the students will need longer to complete them. Group work on tasks may be useful as formative activity for students who need to prepare for a test.

Submission size

You will need to make an estimate of how long students need to read and complete each question, then work out how many can be answered in the time available for the examination. It is a good idea to test some sample questions with students, to get an idea of how many questions you can reasonably include in a test.

Timing

Examinations can be set at any time after a certain amount of knowledge has been taught, but, for practical reasons, such as availability of large, secure spaces and of invigilators, they are often scheduled at the end of a module or course.

Inclusive practice

Like all unseen exams, this type of task tests the ability to work under a time constraint and can be very stressful for students. It may favour students with particular personalities and previous experiences of success in similar situations, and disadvantage students who are prone to anxiety. It is worth considering whether they achieve your intended purposes for the task: unseen exams are an artificial situation which students are unlikely to encounter outside education. For these reasons, they are best used as part of a varied assessment strategy to allow students to demonstrate their ability in a range of situations.

Students who need extra time for reading will need arrangements to be made in advance. Sometimes, students with severe anxiety may need to take their examination in a room apart from other students. There also need to be arrangements for students to use the bathroom when needed. These arrangements will usually be made by professional services teams in the university on a consistent basis for all courses, but if you are managing an unseen examination in your own class time, you will need to think about these things.

Avoiding academic misconduct

This kind of task is usually under exam conditions, using answers provided to the students, so you shouldn't need to worry about plagiarism or cheating.

Oral examination

Description

An oral examination is a form of assessment that tests the ability to respond verbally under time constraints. Oral examinations can be used to present an idea or position, as a supplement to a related assessment, such as the production of an artefact or research proposal, to elaborate on or justify decisions made in a particular situation, or to simulate a situation, such as meeting with a client or an interview as part of a job application process. This format also includes an oral examination or viva.

A twist on the interview task is to ask the students to prepare to interview someone else, but in this case you are testing their ability to interview rather than to respond to unprepared questions.

Level

Oral examinations as summative assessment will work better at higher levels, when students have started to develop an ability to synthesise information and respond to prompts, challenges, and questions. Use at levels 5–7.

Indicative learning outcomes

On completion of this task, students will be able to:

- Present information about [topic area] to a defined audience
- Explain how they have developed skills in [relevant area] with reference to their future professional development plans
- Prepare appropriate questions for a professional interview with a prospective candidate for a job in their field

Key information

The focus of the examinations needs to be clear and students need to have some idea of what to prepare in advance. You need to decide whether you will allow the student to bring in notes or not. The examinations need to be planned in outline in advance, to ensure that each student is asked questions of a similar number, level, and relevance. This is just to provide an overall structure; it doesn't preclude your following up individual responses with questions that are tailored to the student, which will give you a better picture of their ability to respond under these conditions. You could share with the students in advance the basic questions that might be asked, to give them an idea of what to prepare.

If you are assessing specific skills, then an analytical marking scheme that is focused on small tasks will work best. A clear analytical scheme will also help the examiner to make quick and accurate decisions about the student's performance on that task and should help with consistency between assessors: you are likely to need multiple assessors to complete these exams for a big group. Each task may be assessed on a pass/refer basis, or graded. The final mark would usually be based on a total of the marks. The examiner usually marks the student performance on the spot, and then the marks from each station are combined to make a grade for the whole examination.

As for all event-based assessments, it is a good idea to have two assessors present, who should consider marks and feedback independently before conferring to agree a final grade after the assessment. If this is not possible, you should record all, or a sample, of the interviews for moderation.

Student choice

There is not much opportunity for student choice in this kind of assignment, unless you take the option of assessing the students' ability to interview someone else, rather than being interviewed.

Suitability for groups

It is possible to interview a pair or a group, but it is easier to judge the student rather than their contribution to a group answer if the examination is carried out with individuals.

Submission size

How long might you need to assess the learning outcomes? Five to ten minutes might be sufficient to support a research proposal, or 20 minutes for a simulated job interview. You need to think about the amount of time you actually have available, the number of assessors, and the number of students to be assessed.

Timing

An oral assessment or interview can be set at any time in the module or programme, as long as students have enough time to prepare themselves.

Inclusive practice

This kind of assignment can be stressful; students will find it helpful if you explain exactly what will happen during the interview and give them opportunities to practise. However, they can be very valuable for students who try to avoid such situations but who will need to engage with interviews to progress in their professional lives. Giving students opportunities to share their anxieties and to prepare with practice interviews will help to make these assessments less challenging.

For students who have difficulties with speech or hearing, this is an opportunity to discuss alternatives that they can then share with future employers. You might need to provide questions in advance so that they can prepare written answers.

Avoiding academic misconduct

It is difficult for students to conduct an entire interview using the words of others, and you can reduce the risk by modifying the line of questioning, depending on their responses. To reduce the risks of students who are scheduled later in the process being able to prepare answers, you should not ask the same questions of each student; you will need to have a small bank of questions available. However, you need to ask similar levels of questions to each person.

Presentation

Description

A presentation is a task in which students present a synthesis of a topic to a defined audience, usually verbally. It is in the examination section as it is usually done live, either in person or via video conferencing, with the opportunity for the audience to ask questions. You could ask for a recording, which would make it coursework: the considerations would be the same for either, but you might expect more polish for a recording, as students could repeat until they are satisfied with the results, and there wouldn't be a possibility to ask questions live.

Students can use presentations to report research findings, introduce a new curriculum topic to their peers, to reflect on experiences, to suggest just a few possible applications. Most programmes will include presentations as an assessment requirement at all levels, in order to give students practice at speaking to an audience.

Level

Presentations can be set at any level, but the context should get progressively more challenging. At levels 3 and 4 you might ask students to present to a small group of peers, while at levels 6 and 7 the audience could be larger and include some professionals.

Indicative learning outcomes

On completion of this task, students will be able to:

- Summarise a topic in a way suitable for the general public, using relevant literature
- Explain the rationale for a project to an audience of their peers

Key information

You need to be clear about the purpose of the presentation and the intended audience. If a student is presenting the findings of a case study, do you want it to be as if to an audience in the workplace, or as an academic report? If one of the main purposes is to get students to produce a group product, then do you want them to talk in the presentation about how they worked together, or would you like that as a separate written report?

You can assess the presentation using tutor's marks alone, or you can also include an element of peer assessment. As with all event-based marking, consider whether you need to have two assessors present who should complete the mark sheet independently before conferring to agree a final grade after the assessment, or whether you can sample the marking with random checks from a moderator. If the subject of the presentation has an external element (e.g. using a case study from practice or on a new technique), this may be a good opportunity to involve employers or alumni in the assessment process.

You need to decide whether to give marks for the quality of any audiovisual materials or handouts, and for presentation skills, as well as for the content. You also need to be clear about whether or not you are going to penalise presenters who exceed or undershoot the time allowance.

Student choice

You can offer choice over the topic and how the presentation is structured, as well as over the use of audiovisual materials.

Suitability for groups

Presentations often lend themselves well to group work as it is possible for work to be divided up by sharing out the research and analysis, or by taking on roles such as research, slide preparation, and presentation. If students take on different roles, they will need to be encouraged to vary their roles during their academic careers so that they gain experience in a range of tasks.

Submission size

You need to take into account the time available for the assessment and the size of any groups. Individual presentations of more than five minutes can be difficult to assess in terms of scale; even at that length you would only get through around 8–10 students per hour, allowing for changeovers. Ten minutes for a group of 4–5 is a fairly common length of presentation; this might account for 30–40% of the assessment of a unit, probably accompanied by some supplementary written materials, such as a handout or a short reflection on the process of preparation.

Timing

Presentations can happen at any point in a module: early on, students might describe work in progress, and later, they may be synthesising their findings for the audience.

Inclusive practice

Like all time-constrained tasks, this kind of assignment can be stressful; students may find it helpful if you explain exactly what will happen during the presentation and give them opportunities to practise. They also need to see in the marking criteria how important their presentation skills are, compared to their knowledge and understanding, and whether you will penalise them if they freeze on the day. Students with severe anxiety may need an alternative assessment, or be allowed to prepare a video of their presentation.

Avoiding academic misconduct

The presentation is usually planned in advance, so plagiarism can be an issue in the same way as it may be for written assignments. You can reduce the plagiarism potential by relating the presentation title to topical issues, asking for plans at various stages in the term and discussing the content of the presentation in seminars. Asking questions after the presentation also gives you the chance to probe the solidity of the student learning. You could ask students to prepare a presentation under examination conditions, giving them a fixed period of time to prepare it under supervision, but this is likely to be a fairly stressful experience for them, so only use it if you think it will really allow them to demonstrate essential learning outcomes.

Performance or show

Description

Students can use performances or shows to demonstrate a synthesis of their creative work. They are most commonly used in creative disciplines, such as art, design, drama, music, and dance, but there is no reason why they can't be used in other areas.

A performance or show brings together student work into a production which showcases their achievements. Performances can include live poetry, acting, dance, fashion, and/or music, or be exhibitions which are installed to show artwork in a static format, including paintings, film, fashion, textiles, audio, or other work. While performances or shows are common in creative disciplines, you can also use them in other subject areas to encourage creative thinking about problems or knowledge.

Level

While simple performances or shows can be assessed at lower levels, they are often used to showcase professional-quality work at levels 6–7. If you are using this outside conventionally expected creative disciplines, you might use them at lower levels as they will count less towards the final qualifications, which may mean there is less pressure for students.

Indicative learning outcomes

On completion of this task, students will be able to:

- Present a body of work to [a defined audience] using a range of techniques and research
- Work in a team to produce a professional quality of performance or show [in the discipline]

Key information

You need to be clear about the purpose of the performance or show and the actual or intended audience in relation to the learning outcomes of the module. If a student is presenting research findings, will the performance be sufficient, or do you want to see supporting information, such as a logbook or work in progress? If one of the main purposes is to get students to produce a group product, do you want them to explain how they worked together, and if so, should they do this in a separate submission?

You can assess the presentation using teacher marks alone, or you can also include an element of peer assessment. For this kind of event-based assessment, I would recommend having two assessors present who should complete the mark sheet independently before conferring to agree a final grade after the assessment. There may be an opportunity to involve the audience, or visitors to the show, in the assessment process. This could include potential employers. Additionally, or alternatively, depending on context, the students could be asked to reflect on feedback from the audience or visitors.

You need to decide whether to give marks for the quality of the presentations of the performance or show, as well as for the content. You also need to be clear if you are going to penalise presenters who exceed or undershoot time or space allowances.

Student choice

There are many possibilities for student choice here. They can choose the theme, who they work with, and what roles they play in a group. This can be overwhelming, so you may also want to support their decision-making with regular discussion about the work, and peer review of work in progress.

Suitability for groups

Performances and shows often lend themselves well to group work, as it is possible for work to be divided up by sharing out contributions, or by taking on roles in relation to design, production, and performance. There may be many roles available and students may have the chance to demonstrate their strengths by choosing roles they know they do well, or to experiment in other roles; they may need to be encouraged to try out different roles during their academic careers so that they gain experience in a range of tasks.

You need to decide whether to give marks to individual roles or to assess the group as a whole. For a complex production like a play or opera, it may be difficult to decide how to allocate grades across roles, so it may be easier to give a group mark, but ask the students to weight individual contributions.

Submission size

You need to take into account the time needed for the assessment and the size of any groups. How long do you need to spend on making assessments of individual contributions or performances, or installations in a show? How many can you realistically judge accurately in one session? There will be disciplinary norms or expectations in creative disciplines. For those in other subject areas, think about the usual length of presentations as a rough guide to what you might expect from these types of tasks.

Timing

Big productions are usually at the end of a programme, and may count for a large proportion of credits for the year.

Inclusive practice

A complex group production should have roles available for everyone, whatever they are bringing to the task. The challenge will be to allocate these roles equitably. You can support this by having open discussion about individual strengths and contributions, and ensuring that all roles are equally valued.

Although students will have had a lot of time to prepare, the final performance or show is still constrained by time and space, and so, like all examination-type assignments, students may feel pressure. You can support them by reviewing work in progress and making sure that they understand what will happen when the work is assessed.

Avoiding academic misconduct

If the presentation is used to present disciplinary content, then plagiarism could be an issue, as it may be for written assignments. You can reduce the plagiarism potential by asking for plans at various stages in the term and discussing the work with students at regular intervals, as well as on the day of the performance or show.

Reference

QAA. (2008). *The framework for higher education qualifications in England, Wales and Northern Ireland (FHEQ)*. London: Quality Assurance Agency for Higher Education.

11
FEEDBACK TOOLS

This section describes some commonly used approaches to feedback and some of the advantages and disadvantages of their use. Of course, you will think of more interesting variations on any of these, and develop them, but combined with the design considerations in Chapter 6 and the practical implementation of feedback in Chapter 8, they are intended to help you select a general approach quickly and confidently.

You can combine different approaches in your overall feedback planning for the module; some ideas for this are included, but please don't treat these as a prescription.

Generic feedback

Description

Generic feedback is produced to be suitable for the whole class, picking out common strengths, weaknesses, and suggestions for future work from which everyone might benefit.

Key information

Generic feedback can be presented verbally in class or provided digitally in audio or written format. It should be concise, reiterating your initial expectations, summarising a selection of successful elements and common problems and how they might have been avoided. If you use generic feedback part-way through the module, you can adapt teaching for the rest of the module to cover areas which need development, and show explicitly how you use what you have learned from marking the work to support student improvement.

Generic feedback should always be anonymised: never use actual examples of students' work, even if they were excellent. There may be other places to highlight outstanding work, but the purpose of generic feedback is to enable everyone to improve, and this is difficult if there is focus on individual examples.

In terms of timing, it is probably best not to release generic feedback before everyone has submitted: if a student has an extension, they may get an advantage from hearing your thoughts on the submissions of others.

Reasons to choose this approach

- You want to give early feedback to the group as a whole, before returning individually marked assignments
- You want to highlight the group's achievements as a whole
- There are common issues to address across the group
- You want to provide a brief overview to colleagues as well as students

Advantages

It is quick to produce, being a summary of your overall reflections; you can even produce it after having marked a sample of the group's work. If you present the feedback in class, you may have a captive audience and you can answer questions about it, so creating more of a dialogue, rather than the feedback being one way. Colleagues who teach the same students in a future module, or who will be teaching this module in the future, will find a short summary like this really useful for developing their own teaching.

Slightly paradoxically, it can be an advantage that it is depersonalised: individual students don't have an emotional engagement with the feedback, which may make it easier for them to work with it.

Disadvantages

It is impersonal: some students may think it doesn't apply to them. It does not show how individual marks were achieved

Can be combined with

Generic feedback can be combined with: marking rubric; annotations on submission; face-to-face meeting; automated feedback.

Marking rubric

Description

You highlight areas on your marking rubric to show how the grading decisions were made.

Key information

Many digital coursework submission tools will allow you to attach a rubric to an assignment task and then highlight the boxes where students have achieved, but a printed copy and a highlighter pen also still work, although you will then need a system to return the rubric to the students. All that you are doing here is showing how the final mark was achieved, so this wouldn't be feedback students can easily act on; it should be supplemented with personalised feed-forward if possible.

Reasons to choose this approach

- There are several teachers marking the work and you are aiming for consistency of presentation
- You want to focus on feed-forward comments
- You want a clear way to justify the grades

Advantages

The rubric also helps moderators to see what decisions you made during marking, and it is relatively quick to highlight areas on the rubric while you are marking.

Disadvantages

It is impersonal, and all that you are doing here is showing how the final mark was achieved, so this wouldn't be feedback students can easily act on; for both reasons, it should be supplemented with personalised feed-forward if possible.

Can be combined with

Marking rubric can be combined with: feedback sheet; audio or video file; annotations on submission; face-to-face meeting.

Feedback sheet

Description

A feedback sheet is a standardised form that allows you to highlight strengths and weaknesses of the submission, and possibly add some short, personalised feedback at the end.

Key information

You could use the marking rubric as the main part of the form, and then add some more open headings, such as 'three strengths; three things to work on in your next assignment'.

Reasons to choose this approach

- It is quick to complete
- It focuses on key aspects of the submission
- It is consistent in terms of type and amount of feedback

Advantages

These forms are usually quick to complete and are likely to offer some consistency across assignments and across markers. If all teachers on a course use the same form, the standard approach may make comparisons between assignment tasks easier for students and moderators.

Disadvantages

The feedback is impersonal, even with the additional comments, and students may find it difficult to relate generic comments to their work. Combining this with annotations on submission, or the offer of a face-to-face meeting, might mitigate this and help to make feedback more useful.

Can be combined with

Feedback sheets can be combined with: marking rubric; annotations on submission; face-to-face meetings.

Audio or video file

Description

An audio or video file would be used in the same way as a written feedback sheet: a digital file which is provided to the students summarising your comments.

Key information

Most digital assignment management systems will support uploading or creating audio or video files as feedback. It is better if they allow you to create from within the system, as then each file will be automatically associated with the student submission. However, you may need to produce the files separately, in which case you need a clear naming and filing system to make sure that you upload them to the correct student account. You will also need to delete the files from your own device once you have uploaded them, so that you are not storing unnecessary personal information.

You can use audio to provide spoken feedback, which can make it feel more personal to the student. You can add video so that they can see you as well as hear you, or you can use screen capture software to show you looking at a digital submission, with the option of a voiceover of you talking through your questions and comments about different elements of the submission.

Reasons to choose this approach

- You want to ensure your tone of voice is captured
- You or your students prefer speaking and listening to writing and reading
- You want to make specific points which are better presented in one of these formats
- You type slowly

Advantages

This can feel quite personalised to students. You can use such feedback to provide a holistic view of the assignment, or you can focus on individual aspects; screen capture is really useful to point to specific parts of a text or a digital artefact, such as a map, diagram, or artwork.

Disadvantages

Production and management of files can be time-consuming, especially if they are not built into the assignment submission system. Audio, video, and screen capture production are not such commonplace skills as word-processing, so you may need to undertake additional training before using these.

Can be combined with

Audio or video file can be combined with: marking rubric; annotations on submission.

Annotations on submission

Description

Annotations are added to student work to make points about specific locations in the work.

Key information

Annotations can of course be handwritten on printed submissions, if you still work with these. You can also use a tool for commenting or track changes, such as those built into most commonly used word-processing software or in an online marking tool. With these, you can usually add comments or edit text; personally, I prefer to use comments rather than edit a student's text directly, as this makes it clearer that this is a judgement on an individual completed submission, rather than a collaborative editing process. I also use a question format for comments, for instance: 'Have you thought about?'; 'Is this the only way to interpret that paper?'; 'Would someone [in a different situation] ask a different question?'.

You need to decide in advance what kinds of things you will annotate and how much annotation to provide. For instance, will you note errors in grammar, punctuation, and spelling, and if so, will you point all of them out, or a selection? Will you direct students to other sources of help, such as library or study skills resources, in the comments?

Reasons to choose this approach

- It is a formative submission
- Students will be producing something similar in the near future and will benefit from detailed comments

Advantages

This approach enables you to share the way you were thinking as you were reading through the submission. This can help students to understand the points in the submission where they could have been more critical, there are errors in reasoning or calculations, or the structure needs attention because, for instance, you had a question that actually gets answered later on.

Disadvantages

Annotations can be time-consuming to produce. They may be pored over and read out of context ('you commented on my use of x on p. 3, but not on p. 7'), so you need to be clear about how you expect students to use them. They will not show the students exactly how their mark was achieved, but this shouldn't be the focus of the feedback anyway (see Chapter 6).

Can be combined with

Annotations of submission can be combined with: generic feedback; marking rubric; face-to-face meeting.

Face-to-face meeting

Description

This is a scheduled meeting to focus on feedback with individual students, or with a group if it was a group submission,

Key information

You can use a face-to-face session as the main way to present the feedback, or as an optional supplement to another type of feedback, so that students come and ask you questions about the feedback they have received in another format. Whichever you choose, you will need to have prepared brief notes or bullet points for each student to help you remember your main thoughts about their submission. Meetings can be held in person or online – you could offer students a choice, so that those who find it difficult to come to campus for ad-hoc meetings are able to take up the opportunity.

If you are using this as the main way to present feedback, you need to make sure that you allow time to elicit and answer questions from the student, so that it isn't just a mini-presentation of the feedback, which could be done with a video or audio file. You also need to think about whether you mind if students don't attend a scheduled meeting. These meetings may be scheduled after a module has finished, so students may not have the motivation or time to attend. Does this matter? As we have previously discussed, many students don't collect or read feedback provided in other formats, but this will make the situation more visible to you.

Reasons to choose this approach

- You want to be certain that students understand the feedback
- You have a first submission part-way through a module, which will be built on for a final assignment task: it's an opportunity to clarify and motivate students for the next submission
- You are working closely with a student on a project or dissertation
- You want to develop your relationship with students

Advantages

A dialogue is very personal, and it gives you a chance to identify misunderstandings and concerns immediately, and to encourage students to focus on their next actions.

Disadvantages

This may not be practical if you have very large groups. Even if you only allow ten minutes per student, you will only reasonably manage to see five students per hour. However, you could balance the time for this against the time needed to produce more detailed feedback in another format.

Verbal feedback may not show the students exactly how their mark was achieved, but this shouldn't be the focus of the feedback anyway (see Chapter 6).

Can be combined with

Face-to-face meeting can be combined with: marking rubric; feedback sheet; annotations on submission.

Automated feedback

Description

Automated feedback is linked to a submission using a pre-prepared computer process.

Key information

Such feedback would usually be provided alongside the results of a computer-marked test.

Reasons to choose this approach

- You are using computer-marked exams
- Students are working independently
- Submissions are made at different times in the module or course, perhaps formatively

Advantages

Feedback is received immediately and this may make it more likely that students are able to act on it. There is no need for the tutor to do anything at the time of marking. The feedback is linked directly to a particular question, so shows how the mark was achieved.

Disadvantages

The main disadvantage is the time needed to set up useful feedback for every alternative on a computer-marked exam. For multiple-choice questions, each distractor needs individual feedback to explain why it wasn't the best answer. For short-answer questions, you need to predict a range of possible incorrect answers, or just provide the correct answer – which may not help students to see where they have gone wrong. The feedback is impersonal, which may reduce engagement.

Can be combined with

Automated feedback can be combined with: generic feedback.

GLOSSARY

Assessment task the work to be undertaken by a student and submitted for evaluation by a teacher. The task can be formative or summative.

Assignment brief the description of the task to be undertaken by a student. This should include the intended learning outcomes, the expected size of the work which is submitted, how many credits are associated with the task, how it will be graded, what feedback will be provided, and how that feedback should be used.

Award the qualification or certification associated with a complete course or programme of study.

Contract cheating the practice of a student paying someone else to produce an assignment, and then submitting it as if they had completed it themselves.

Course the overall description of the requirements for an award, including the overall aims, the different modules which may be taken to complete it, any practical or placement elements, and the duration of study. In this book, the words 'programme' and 'course' are used interchangeably, but this may differ according to country and institution.

Coursework an assessment task which is completed during the time of a module at the student's own pace and in a place of their choosing, and usually with access to any resources chosen by the student.

Credit a measure of the value of an assignment task in relation to a complete award. In the UK, a bachelor's degree is worth a total of 360 credits (equivalent to 180 credits on the European Credit Transfer System, ECTS). Each module on a course will have a credit rating which shows how much it contributes to the overall award.

Examination an assessment task which must be completed during a specific period of time, and which may have other constraints, such as to be taken in a specific place with specified resources available.

Examiner the person who judges the student achievement on a particular submission.

Fairness the extent to which all students have an equal opportunity to demonstrate their achievement of the intended outcomes.

Feedback commentary provided to the student about how well they have completed this task and what they should do to improve their performance in future assessment tasks.

Formative assessment assessment which does not count for module credits.

Intended learning outcomes a description of what a student will be able to do at the end of a programme of study.

Invigilator the person who ensures that an examination is conducted in accordance with the constraints which have been decided and any university regulations which also apply. Usually, the invigilator would be unconnected to the course or module team. In some countries, the term 'proctor' is used instead.

Mitigations changes to an assessment task or procedures which are intended to mitigate against disadvantage caused by an individual student situation (e.g. illness) or a general problem (e.g. tutor illness, or disruption due to a pandemic).

Moderation the critical peer review of assessment processes and procedures, including review of a sample of student submissions, which can be completed at module or programme level.

Moderator the person who reviews assessment processes, tasks, and submissions, and provides feedback on consistency and standards. A moderator can be internal to the university, or external (in this case, they may be called external examiners).

Module a discrete part of a course or programme of study which has specific intended learning outcomes and assessment tasks.

Plagiarism the act of presenting someone else's ideas or work as your own.

Proctor see Invigilator.

Programme of study the overall description of the requirements for an award, including the overall aims, the different modules which may be taken to complete it, any practical or placement elements, and the duration of study. In this book, the words 'programme' and 'course' are used interchangeably, but this may differ according to country and institution.

Reliability the extent to which a process leads to the same outcomes when it is repeated. This is difficult to measure for assessment tasks in a higher education context where students are producing unique, open-ended work with a high degree of criticality and creativity, and are not expected to submit similar work. Reliability of examiners is evaluated by the use of moderation strategies.

Remote proctoring the process of carrying out invigilation or proctoring online. For instance, if a student is taking an examination in an environment which is not controlled by the university, they may be observed via web camera.

Stakes a term commonly used to indicate the importance of an assessment task. A high stakes task represents a higher proportion of the final award, and a low stakes task has less value in relation to the final award. The Credit value of the module will indicate its importance. See also Weighting.

Submission the work which is presented for evaluation.

Summative assessment assessment which is used to determine module credits, as opposed to summative assessment.

Teacher the person responsible for making decisions about assessment and judgements about student achievement.

Validity the extent to which an assessment task measures the intended learning outcomes.

Weighting the proportion of the module or course award which an assessment task represents. For example, a module might have two tasks: one piece of coursework with a weighting of 50%, and one examination with a weighting of 50%. Weighting may also be expressed in terms of the number of Credits associated with the assessment task. See also Stakes.

INDEX